THE GOSPEL OF THE
KINGDOM

STEVE PIXLER

THE GOSPEL OF THE KINGDOM

STEVE PIXLER

THE GOSPEL OF THE KINGDOM | STEVE PIXLER
First Edition

© 2022 by Steve Pixler | All rights reserved

Published by **Continuum Ministry Resources**
Mansfield, TX

Learn more at **stevepixler.com**

Unless otherwise noted, scripture quotations are from New Revised Standard Version Bible, copyright © 1989 National Council of the Churches of Christ in the United States of America. Used by permission. All rights reserved worldwide. nrsvbibles.org

ISBN: 978-0-9914552-7-0

TABLE OF CONTENTS

Introduction   7

Module 1: Introduction to the Gospel of the Kingdom   9

Unit 1: Tracing the History of Kingdom Expectation   11

Unit 2: How Jesus Reframed the Kingdom   17

Unit 3: The Coming of the Spirit & the Kingdom   29

Module 2: The Ascended King   37

Unit 4: The Principalities & Powers   39

Unit 5: Matthew 28: The Great Commission   47

Unit 6: Ephesians 3: The Repatriation of the Nations   59

Module 3: How the Kingdom Comes in the World   71

Unit 7: Personal & Family Transformation   73

Unit 8: Ekklesia   85

Unit 9: Transforming Culture Through Manifest Glory   103

Module 4: Eschatology & Expectation   129

Unit 10: Key Texts That Shape Our Expectation   131

Unit 11: What Do We Expect? Correcting Mistaken Eschatology   153

Unit 12: Final Word   163

INTRODUCTION

This book is the first shot—and scatter-shot, at that!—at a textbook for an online course produced by Steve Pixler and Continuum Ministry Resources, the titanic publishing arm of Continuum Ministries, Inc., Steve Pixler's national, international, worldwide, global and intergalactic ministry.

The course is available at stevepixler.com.

This is a work in progress. The gospel of the kingdom is inexhaustible. By necessity, therefore, any book's attempt to say all that needs to be said is guaranteed to fail. Also by necessity, then, we will update and print future editions as we teach through the material and the gaps become obvious to the meanest intelligence.

You, the reader, the student, the fellow space traveler, will help us do this invaluable updating as we go. As you take the course and interact online with the material, your questions, comments and observations will help us fine tune the content. We deeply appreciate your feedback.

Having said all that, though, this book is pretty good as it is. In fact, it is stupendous. And how can a book help but be stupendous when the topic is of such eternal significance? The gospel of the kingdom is a big deal, and never have we needed this big deal message as much as we need it now. There is a kingdom revolution shaking the world right now, and prophetic people everywhere are echoing the urgency. It is a move of God, and it is meant to move you and me.

As you work through the material, you will discover that the running theme throughout is *audacious faith*. The gospel of the kingdom runs on faith like a combustion engine runs on fuel. Our prayer is that you will be tanked up with world-changing faith, the kind of faith that emboldens you to devote your life from this day forward to advancing the rule of King Jesus in every realm of life.

Now, pull on your space helmet and let's get started.

MODULE 1: INTRODUCTION TO THE GOSPEL OF THE KINGDOM

UNIT 1: TRACING THE HISTORY OF KINGDOM EXPECTATION

There are two things to know immediately.

First, the word "gospel" comes from the Greek word *"euangelion,"* and it means "good news." In ancient Greek and Roman usage, *euangelion* was used to announce the accession of a king to his throne, which was heralded to the citizens of the realm as "good news."

Second, the word "kingdom" comes from the Greek word *"basileia,"* which was the palace or seat of government of a king. A "basilica" was an ancient Roman government building where citizens gathered and government business was conducted. The idea of "basilica" was carried over into institutional Christianity through the design of church buildings that imitates the design of ancient Roman basilicas.

So, "the gospel of the kingdom"—the *euangelion* of the *basileia*—in the New Testament is first of all the good news announcement that God is King of all creation and that Jesus, His Son, has ascended to the throne of his Father as the new Adam, as Messiah, the Son of David.

The gospel of the kingdom is described both as "the kingdom of God" and "the kingdom of heaven." Though these are interchangeable terms, "the kingdom of God" phrase emphasizes the rule of the triune God over all creation in cooperation with humans, and the phrase "the kingdom of heaven" emphasizes the transcendent culture of the heavens breaking in upon the fallen earth. "The kingdom of God" emphasizes the "person" of the King and his people, while "the kingdom of heaven" emphasizes the transcendent "place" from beyond that is breaking into the world through the Spirit-indwelled people.

The kingdom of God is simply God's rule over all creation in cooperation with humans. But over time, the idea of the kingdom took on eschatological significance within biblical history. So when Jesus came preaching "the gospel of the kingdom," it meant something profoundly specific to Israel. It is what the kingdom meant to Israel and came to mean to the church that we will explore in this course.

Where did the kingdom of God within history originate?

It started in the Garden of Eden when God gave Adam and Eve *the dominion mandate.* (Genesis 1:26-31) Though kingdom language is not used explicitly, the idea of divine-human collaboration in the rule over creation is implicit. However, Psalm 8 makes the dominion/kingdom idea explicit:

When I look at your heavens, the work of your fingers, the moon and the stars that you have established; what are human beings that you are mindful of them, mortals that you care for them? Yet you have made them a little lower than God, and crowned them with glory and honor. You have given them dominion over the works of your hands; you have put all things under their feet. (Psalm 8:3–6, NRSV)

God "crowned them with glory and honor." This is kingdom language.

The idea of ruling with God is also implicit in the Abrahamic covenant. (Genesis 12, 13, 15, 17) But it is only when Israel is gathered at Sinai that the people of God are first called "a kingdom of priests" and formally, officially constituted as God's chosen nation among all the nations.

Now therefore, if you obey my voice and keep my covenant, you shall be my treasured possession out of all the peoples. Indeed, the whole earth is mine, but you shall be for me a priestly kingdom and a holy nation. These are the words that you shall speak to the Israelites." (Exodus 19:5–6, NRSV)

The next iteration of the kingdom was the Davidic Kingdom under David and Solomon, the Golden Age of Israel. For eighty years, Israel prospered under their rule, and God made a covenant with David that his lineage would always be seated on Israel's throne. The "House of David" became the kingly dynasty that was promised to rule forever. David and Solomon built Jerusalem, "the city" and "the temple" as the dwelling place of God, which are recurring themes of the kingdom of God, as we shall see.

However, Israel turned away from the worship of the one true God, and they were sent into exile just as Moses predicted so long ago. The Exile was the most devastating event in Israel's history up to that time, and the prophets responded to the disaster by predicting the restoration of the kingdom through the return of the Son of David, the Anointed One, the One later called "The Messiah."

A quick survey of the prophets shows that they all predicted Israel's return from exile and restoration in the land. The city and temple would be rebuilt and the presence of God would return. The enemies of Israel would all be defeated and Israel would become the head of the nations. Through Israel's restoration—the restoration of David's kingdom in the rule of Messiah—all the nations of the earth come to worship the one true God, thus fulfilling the covenant made with Abraham that all nations of the earth would be blessed though his offspring.

Though all the pre-exilic prophets foretold the Jewish diaspora, Jeremiah was the most specific. In Jeremiah 29, the prophet foretold seventy years of captivity at the hands of the Babylonians. Then, he promised that God would return Israel to their land and restore the Davidic kingdom. It was this promise that Daniel was reading (Daniel 9) when he implored the Lord to fulfill his promise and end exile forever.

However, an angel was sent to Daniel to inform him that the seventy years of captivity had been extended (due to lack of true repentance, as Moses predicted) to "Seventy Weeks." In prophetic time, the Seventy Weeks are understood as weeks of years, which adds up to 490 years. Daniel was shown that there would be 490 years from the decree of Cyrus to rebuild the city and temple until the coming of "one like a Son of Man" and the restoration of the kingdom to "the saints" by "the Ancient of Days." (Daniel 7)

During the "Intertestamental Period" (roughly 400 years between Malachi and Matthew), faithful Jews studied Daniel and the apocryphal writings that explored the timeline of Messiah's appearance and Israel's restoration. By the time Jesus came preaching the gospel of the kingdom, expectations were running high in Israel concerning Messiah's advent. This is why Jesus said:

> "The time is fulfilled, and the kingdom of God has come near; repent, and believe in the good news." (Mark 1:15, NRSV)

"The time" to which Jesus referred as "fulfilled" was the time predicted by Daniel. The idea that the time had come was no surprise to Israel. Everyone in Jesus' day was talking about it. From the religious leaders in Jerusalem to Herod's palace to peasants on the street, everyone was discussing the coming of Messiah. In fact, there were many false messianic appearances in the first and second centuries, all of them due to the heightened kingdom expectation.

The announcement that the time of the kingdom had come was no surprise. However, *how* Jesus announced the kingdom did bring considerable shock to those who heard him. Israel, due to all the prophets promised, expected Messiah to lead Israel in a military and political victory against her enemies (which were the Romans in the first century), and restore by force Israel to the head of the nations.

In the next unit, let's look at how Jesus reframed the kingdom and blew Israel's expectations out of the water.

UNIT 2: HOW JESUS REFRAMED THE KINGDOM

Israel in the first century had three primary expectations regarding the kingdom—more specifically, regarding the coming of Messiah, which would inaugurate the kingdom, as they saw it.

1. **The Temple:** Faithful Jews believed that Messiah would cleanse the temple and restore purified worship to Israel, reconsecrating and reestablishing the pure Levitical priesthood as Ezekiel promised. The Pharisees (their name meant "the separated ones"), the Essenes, the Zealots and other religious puritans of the day despised the corrupt Sadducees who ran the temple complex in collusion with the hated Romans.

2. **The City:** Faithful Jews believed that Messiah would enter Jerusalem by the Eastern Gate (Ezekiel 43:2), deliver the city from the Romans and restore it to its Davidic glory as the capital of the restored kingdom.

3. **The Nation:** Faithful Jews believed that Messiah would elevate Israel to the head of the nations and lead all the nations to worship the one true God, following Israel's inspired example.

These expectations were not drawn from thin air. Israel's prophets had foretold each of these things. For centuries, Israel had clung to the hope that God would rend the heavens and come down to set things right once for all. The prophets foretold that "the Son of Man," the figure that faithful Jews came to describe as "Messiah" (the Anointed One), would come to lead Israel to everlasting victory. Though we don't have space here to present a thorough survey of the prophets, take a moment when you can to skim quickly through the prophets and note how much they spoke about Israel's restoration. It is everywhere.

For almost five centuries, Israel had studied God's promises. Many interpretations of how the promises would be fulfilled drifted through Israel's history, but fundamentally, Israel never lost hope that Messiah would come and do all the prophets foretold.

When Jesus came preaching the gospel of the kingdom, no one was shocked by his announcement —at least, not at first. Everyone was expecting the kingdom. But Jesus started preaching almost immediately about the kingdom in a different way. And that *was* shocking. The difference can be summed up in three statements:

1. *The kingdom comes spiritually*
2. *The kingdom comes gradually*
3. *The kingdom comes fully*

Let's look at each one.

The Kingdom Comes Spiritually

One of the primary misunderstandings of the kingdom that Jesus came to overthrow was the idea that the kingdom would come through violence. A quick read through the prophets makes it clear why Israel expected the kingdom to come through military revolution, but Jesus came to "fulfill the law and the prophets" and show that a fleshly understanding of the law and prophets had seriously misled Israel's expectation. Jesus came to reveal the truth. (John 1:17)

As Jesus put it, the kingdom could only come through a "birth from above":

1 Now there was a Pharisee named Nicodemus, a leader of the Jews. 2 He came to Jesus by night and said to him, "Rabbi, we know that you are a teacher who has come from God; for no one can do these signs that you do apart from the presence of God."

*3 Jesus answered him, "Very truly, I tell you, no one can see the kingdom of God without being **born from above**."*

4 Nicodemus said to him, "How can anyone be born after having grown old? Can one enter a second time into the mother's womb and be born?"

5 Jesus answered, "Very truly, I tell you, no one can enter the kingdom of God without being born of water and Spirit. 6 What is born of the flesh is flesh, and what is born of the Spirit is spirit. 7 Do not be astonished that I said to you, 'You must be born from above.' 8 The wind blows where it chooses, and you hear the sound of it, but you do not know where it comes from or where it goes. So it is with everyone who is born of the Spirit."

9 Nicodemus said to him, "How can these things be?" 10 Jesus answered him, "Are you a teacher of Israel, and yet you do not understand these things? (John 3:1–10, NRSV)

The kingdom could only come by taking root in regenerated human hearts and flowing out into a Spirit-transformed world. As Jesus told the astonished Pharisees, who asked when the kingdom of God was coming, "The kingdom of God is not coming with things that can be observed; nor will they say, 'Look, here it is!' or 'There it is!' For, in fact, the kingdom of God is among (within) you" (Luke 17:20–21, NRSV). Paul echoed the same idea when he wrote to the church at Rome, "For the kingdom of God is not food and drink but righteousness and peace and joy in the Holy Spirit" (Romans 14:17, NRSV).

The kingdom of God is *"in the Holy Spirit."*

Jesus and Paul were correcting a fundamental misunderstanding of the kingdom that the law and the prophets had intensified throughout Israel's history: "Flesh and blood cannot inherit the kingdom of God, nor does the perishable inherit the imperishable" (1 Corinthians 15:50, NRSV). Israel mistakenly believed that they would inherit the kingdom due to their fleshly lineage traced back to Abraham, fleshly righteousness through the works of the law and fleshly power through military triumph.

This fed the perennial human delusion that the divine can be accessed through human effort outside of union with God. That was the first lie ever told—"you will be like gods, knowing good and evil"—and it was still the underlying lie that corrupted all human religion. Jesus came to expose the lie and make it clear that the rule of God in synergy with humans could happen only through people being filled with the fullness of God.

Jesus shocked Pilate with his "otherworldly" vision of the kingdom:

> *Jesus answered, "My kingdom is not from this world. If my kingdom were from this world, my followers would be fighting to keep me from being handed over to the Jews. But as it is, my kingdom is not from here." (John 18:36, NRSV)*

The kingdom of God does not arise from within the world and its religious, political, military, economic or social systems. However, it is important to make it clear that the kingdom *does* influence each of these areas of human society—it simply does not arise *from* them. The kingdom is not *from* the world, but it does come *into* the world.

It is important to emphasize this fact lest we end up "spiritualizing" the kingdom and reduce it down to an internal, pietistic experience that has no impact on the world. No, the kingdom may not be *from* the world, but it does impact the world. The kingdom is salt and light that transforms the world.

The kingdom of God comes *spiritually*.

The Kingdom Comes Gradually

Due to the timeline Daniel predicted, Israel expected that the kingdom of God would "appear immediately." Here's how Luke recorded it:

> *As they were listening to this, he went on to tell a parable, because he was near Jerusalem, and because they supposed that the kingdom of God was to appear immediately. (Luke 19:11, NRSV)*

Jesus not only wanted them to understand that the kingdom had already appeared "spiritually" through his incarnation and would continue to manifest "spiritually" when the promised Holy Spirit was poured out at Pentecost, but also that the physical manifestation of the kingdom in the earth would be a slow, gradual process.

The kingdom, as Jesus explained it, would come through "born-from-above" people who were filled with the Spirit and allowed the Spirit to flow out of them and transform the world, one person at a time. That is the only way the kingdom can come.

Jesus taught in Matthew 13 that the kingdom of God comes when "the word of the kingdom" takes root like good seed in the hearts of people and grows exponentially until a harvest of righteousness fills the earth. Jesus used the parables of the sower, the wheat and the tares, the mustard seed, the yeast in the dough, treasure in a field, a pearl of great price and the net cast into the sea to show how the kingdom comes. Two of these parables, the mustard seed and the yeast in the dough, are profoundly important to understanding how gradually the kingdom comes and the extent of kingdom victory (which we shall consider in the next section).

Take a quick look at both parables:

He put before them another parable: "The kingdom of heaven is like a mustard seed that someone took and sowed in his field; it is the smallest of all the seeds, but when it has grown it is the greatest of shrubs and becomes a tree, so that the birds of the air come and make nests in its branches."

He told them another parable: "The kingdom of heaven is like yeast that a woman took and mixed in with three measures of flour until all of it was leavened." (Matthew 13:31–33, NRSV)

Why does it take so long for the kingdom to come? Because the kingdom comes through people being filled with the Holy Spirit, one heart at a time, rather than God imposing the kingdom on everyone all at once.

The kingdom comes gradually as the power of sin and death is broken through the transforming power of the cross—the cross that demonstrates how grasping power is broken through generous love. The only One with all power refuses to force the kingdom on anyone. Every knee will bow, but they must do so willingly. As Paul said, no one can confess that Jesus is Lord but by the Holy Spirit. (1 Corinthians 12:3)

Jesus refused to become king by force.

When the people saw the sign that he had done, they began to say, "This is indeed the prophet who is to come into the world." When Jesus realized that they were about to come and take him by force to make him king, he withdrew again to the mountain by himself. (John 6:14–15, NRSV)

The kingdom comes through love, not power. And love takes time.

The kingdom comes *gradually*.

The Kingdom Comes Fully

Jesus taught that the kingdom would come *spiritually* and *gradually*, but he also taught that the kingdom would come *fully*. The idea of kingdom *fullness* originates with the dominion mandate first given to humans in Eden:

> *God blessed them, and God said to them, "Be fruitful and multiply, and fill the earth and subdue it; and have dominion over the fish of the sea and over the birds of the air and over every living thing that moves upon the earth." (Genesis 1:28, NRSV)*

God intended for humans to *fill* the earth, subdue it and have dominion. And this fullness, as is made clear throughout Scripture, is much more than just populating the earth, more than stuffing a human in every corner of the globe. No, while it includes populating the earth, fullness has more to do with developing the latent, creative potential of the earth and its inhabitants. As Psalm 24:1 says, "The earth is the Lord's and all that is in it, the world, and those who live in it." The earth and its people belong to the Lord, and he has never been willing to settle for anything less than *all*.

We will look more closely below at fullness and the extent of kingdom victory. But for now, look back at the two parables quoted above that reveal how Jesus felt about how *fully* the kingdom would come in the world:

He put before them another parable: "The kingdom of heaven is like a mustard seed that someone took and sowed in his field; it is the smallest of all the seeds, but when it has grown it is the greatest of shrubs and becomes a tree, so that the birds of the air come and make nests in its branches."

He told them another parable: "The kingdom of heaven is like yeast that a woman took and mixed in with three measures of flour until all of it was leavened." (Matthew 13:31–33, NRSV)

The point of both parables is how small the kingdom begins and how large it becomes. The mustard seed is "the smallest of all the seeds," but it becomes a tree large enough for birds to nest within its branches. And it only takes a small amount of yeast to permeate three measures of flour—and here's the key point!—"until all of it was leavened." *All of it.* That's Jesus' point. The kingdom of God will permeate *all* of the nations of the earth.

Again, we will talk more below about how the kingdom will permeate the entire earth. But for now, we must grasp how Jesus' teaching on the kingdom reframed Israel's expectation. They saw themselves as an elite, elect, exclusive remnant who would receive the kingdom and then influence the nations. The nations would remain outside the covenant, outside the promises, outside the kingdom. Jesus' teaching on the fullness of the kingdom foreshadows

Paul's teaching on the "mystery" of the kingdom, that all nations would be grafted into Abraham's seed and included in the covenant promises. (Ephesians 3)

The kingdom comes *fully*.

Reframing the Temple, City & Nation

Jesus' reframing of the kingdom profoundly shifted Christian expectation regarding the temple, city and nation. As Jesus and the apostles explained further throughout the New Testament Scriptures, the physical (fleshly) temple, city and nation were models—what New Testament writers called "types and shadows"—of the spiritual temple, city and nation that God always had in mind.

Israel's election as the chosen people of God was always meant to facilitate Israel's role as carriers of a heavenly reality that would break into all the earth. The physical temple, city and nation were never the end goal of God's restoration agenda. The goal was always for the temple of God to be a living temple made of people; for the city to be a living city made of people; and for the nation to be a living nation made of *all people* in every nation under heaven. The goal was always for the entire cosmos to become the "habitation of God through the Spirit" (Ephesians 2:22, KJV).

More on all that below.

For now, let's take a closer look at how the coming of the Spirit at Pentecost manifested kingdom reality in the world.

UNIT 3: THE COMING OF THE SPIRIT & THE KINGDOM

Since the kingdom comes *spiritually*, the coming of the Spirit to regenerate human hearts and draw people into union and collaboration with God is profoundly important to the gospel of the kingdom. Jesus spent a significant part of his final moments with his disciples talking about the coming of the Spirit, the *parakletos* who is summoned to come alongside to lead believers into all truth (the truth about God, self and others, as opposed to the lies entrenched within religion). (John 14-17) Remember, as Paul put it, the kingdom is "in the Holy Spirit." Thus the Holy Spirit is the Spirit of the King coming to dwell within believers.

Let's take a closer look at the coming of the Spirit and the kingdom.

The New Humanity

As the prophets foretold, Israel expected that Messiah would come and pour out upon them the Spirit of the living God. (Joel 2, etc) All the prophets testified that the only hope for a perennially backsliding Israel was a new heart, regenerated by the Spirit of God. (Jeremiah 31:31-34; Ezekiel 36:22-32; etc) Without the indwelling presence of God, Israel was sure to keep turning back to idols.

Only the Spirit of God could turn their hearts permanently back to the one true God.

What Israel did not see was that the outpouring of the Spirit would require the death, resurrection and ascension of Messiah. The Spirit could not be given until after Jesus was crucified, resurrected and glorified. (John 7:39) Though Isaiah and others revealed glimpses of the "suffering Servant," Israel missed the full implications of Christ's mission. Since death (mortality) was the root cause of all human sin, it was necessary for Jesus to defeat death to save the world. As Hebrews puts it:

Since, therefore, the children share flesh and blood, he himself likewise shared the same things, so that through death he might destroy the one who has the power of death, that is, the devil, and free those who all their lives were held in slavery by the fear of death. (Hebrews 2:14–15, NRSV)

The Romans were not the ultimate enemy—death was. And the only way to defeat death was to destroy through death the one with the power of death, the devil.

Not only was it necessary for death to be defeated, but Christ had to be glorified in order to omnipresence his Spirit in believers throughout the world. As long as Christ remained on the earth within its time/space continuum, he was the temporal and spatial embodiment of God and could not mediate the presence of God to believers.

Moreover, the gift of the Spirit would be more than just the Spirit of God—it would be the Spirit of the glorified Son of God, "the man, Christ Jesus" (1 Timothy 2:5). The Holy Spirit would be "the Spirit of his Son [sent forth] into our hearts, crying, "Abba! Father!" (Galatians 4:6, NRSV). The Paraclete would proceed from both the divine Spirit of God and the glorified human Spirit of Jesus. (John 14:26; 15:26)

The glorified new humanity of Jesus was the infusion of new image and glory that fallen humans needed. It wasn't enough just to pour out the Spirit of God upon flesh. That had been done before. But humans needed a new humanity. Humans needed the Spirit to dwell *within*, not just *upon*.

So Jesus, the Son of God, descended into human existence as the Son of Man to birth a new way of being human, a new humanity infused with the Spirit of the living God. Thus, when Jesus poured out the Holy Spirit, believers received both the divine Spirit of God the Father and the glorified human Spirit of God the Son.

This new Spirit-infused humanity was the victorious humanness that Jesus had borne from the womb to the tomb, carried into the heavens as the ascended and exalted Christ, and then poured out at Pentecost into believers.

When Jesus ascended into heaven, he became the glorified human interface for divine-human union and communion. Jesus opened the way for God to become one with us and for us to become one with God. Jesus transcended time and space so humans could ascend into heaven to participate within the triune life of God. Jesus invited us into the perichoretic union, the divine circle dance, of the Father, Son and Spirit.

When Jesus ascended, he received the promise of the Spirit as a divine, kingly bequest. Here's how Peter put it on the Day of Pentecost:

Being therefore exalted at the right hand of God, and having received from the Father the promise of the Holy Spirit, he has poured out this that you both see and hear. (Acts 2:33, NRSV)

Jesus was authorized as a glorified human King to pour out the Spirit and invite believers into his kingly rule. When Christ ascended, he was enthroned. And by the Spirit, Christ lifted us up together to be enthroned with him as the body of Christ. The King made us co-kings with him. We have been empowered by the Spirit to rule and reign with Christ forever.

As Paul put it, God the Father "raised us up with [Jesus] and seated us with him in the heavenly places in Christ Jesus" (Ephesians 2:6, NRSV). As we are seated with Christ in the heavens—and "to be seated" means specifically "to be enthroned"—we mediate the presence of the King and his government into the world. We release the kingdom of God.

The Pledge Of Our Inheritance & The Power of the World To Come

Paul described the Holy Spirit as "the pledge of our inheritance" (Ephesians 1:14). Our full inheritance, as Paul explained throughout his writings, is the fully renewed cosmos, which includes the salvation of all nations (*ta ethne*, the Gentiles). As co-heirs with Christ, the singular seed of Abraham, we inherit the world that Abraham was promised. (Romans 4:13)

The Holy Spirit is the "pledge"—the guarantee, the down payment, the earnest money—of that inheritance. This means that the Holy Spirit poured out on Pentecost is God the Father's pledge to Jesus and us that we shall inherit the world. As Paul put it, we were "marked with the seal of the promised Holy Spirit; this is the pledge of our inheritance toward redemption as God's own people, to the praise of his glory" (Ephesians 1:13–14, NRSV).

As we shall see when we talk more about the extent of kingdom victory prior to the Second Coming, Christ's full inheritance is already being realized here and now. Though the full consummation of Christ's inheritance awaits the resurrection when "the creation itself will be set free from its bondage to decay and will obtain the freedom of the glory of the children of God" (Romans 8:21), yet the "down payment" of that inheritance is already being lived out here and now through the Spirit.

This is important. Most Christians postpone the victory of Christ's kingdom until after he returns, but Paul makes it clear that the power of the Holy Spirit, the presence of the resurrected Christ, means that what is coming has already come in a very real sense. As Paul put it in 2 Corinthians 5, the new creation that is coming has already come:

So if anyone is in Christ, there is a new creation: everything old has passed away; see, everything has become new! (2 Corinthians 5:17, NRSV)

We are the new creation in Christ that guarantees new creation in the cosmos. As the writer of Hebrews put it, the Holy Spirit is "the power of the world (age) to come" (Hebrews 6:5, KJV). Do you see what that means? The power of the age to come has already broken into the present through the indwelling power of the Holy Spirit. What is coming has already come. When Jesus rose from the dead in the middle of human history, he grasped the future and pulled it back into the first century. Since he arose, the Holy Spirit has been mediating the world to come into the present world through Spirit-filled people.

This means two things. First, we cannot bring the kingdom into the world here and now without the power of the world to come—the Holy Spirit. Second, we cannot receive the power of the world to come through the Spirit and then postpone the reality of the world to come until it comes in fullness. The fact that we have received the Spirit of the world to come means that we should expect to see the power of the world to come bring kingdom transformation here and now. We must settle for nothing less than everything that we hope for in the world to come.

What will it be like then? Release it now!

Most importantly, understanding the Spirit as the pledge of our inheritance and the power of the world to come means that we cannot be content with a pietized, privatized Holy Spirit experience that quarantines the kingdom within the human heart and has little to no impact on the world at large. No, the Spirit is the down payment on our inheritance, and our inheritance is the nations of the world and a renewed cosmos. We should expect to see the earnest of that inheritance *now*.

In fact, one key insight about the kingdom is that miracles are signs of the age to come. As Jesus said, "But if it is by the finger of God that I cast out the demons, then the kingdom of God has come to you" (Luke 11:20, NRSV). The phrase Jesus used here is literally, "The kingdom of God has *come upon you!*" When Jesus healed the sick, cast out demons and raised the dead, the kingdom of God was crashing in upon them. Jesus was pointing toward the age to come and saying, in no uncertain terms, "Sickness, demons and death are all illegal in the kingdom!" Jesus was pulling the power of the world to come into the present and transforming the world all around him.

We must do the same.

Baptized Into One Body By the Spirit

One more thing about the coming of the Spirit and the kingdom.

The Spirit not only unites us to God in Christ, but he also unites us to one another. We are made to sit *together* with Christ in heavenly places. We can only rule with Christ *together*. As Jesus put it in Luke 22, we must learn how to share life together around the kingdom table before we can rule with him on kingdom thrones.

Paul said:

> *For in the one Spirit we were all baptized into one body—Jews or Greeks, slaves or free—and we were all made to drink of one Spirit. (1 Corinthians 12:13, NRSV)*

The unity of the body is an eschatological function of the Holy Spirit. By one Spirit, we are made one body. (Ephesians 4) As we shall see, that empowers us to function as the *ekklesia*, the parliament of King Jesus, his seat of government in the world, his kingdom training center. More on that below.

MODULE 2: THE ASCENDED KING

UNIT 4: THE PRINCIPALITIES & POWERS

The kingdom comes in the world because Christ the King ascended into heaven and poured out the Holy Spirit, the Spirit of the King, to reign within believers and flow out of them into the world around them. Believers are the portals of heaven into earth. As Jesus taught us to pray, "Let it be on earth as it is in heaven."

The reality of Christ's ascension—the ascension is much more than a "doctrine"!—is fundamental to understanding the gospel of the kingdom. For so many believers, the ascended Christ is "out of sight, out of mind." They focus on his past earthly ministry and his future Second Coming, but they know little about his present work with and through the church in heaven and earth. Other than praying to Christ in heaven, which they often perform as if shouting across a great distance, they know almost nothing of his present, ascended ministry.

Jesus is presently ministering in heaven as our Priest, Prophet and King. He is not inactive, seated on the throne twiddling his thumbs, idly waiting for the day of his return. No, Jesus is actively ministering in the heavenly temple. And we minister with him. In fact, when we talk more about the ekklesia of King Jesus (the church), we will look more closely at how we minister as priests, prophets and kings in collaboration with Christ.

For now, though, let's focus over the next three units on three aspects of Christ's ascension:

1. The Principalities and Powers
2. Matthew 28: The Great Commission
3. Ephesians 3: The Repatriation of the Nations

Understanding the principalities and powers—which we will simplify as "the powers"—is absolutely essential to understanding how the kingdom comes in the world. The Great Commission passage in Matthew 28 will help us understand the authority of Christ and how we cooperate with him to fulfill that authority and disciple the nations. The unit on Ephesians 3 will help us understand Christ's inheritance of all nations and how they are being returned to the Father through Christ's mediatorial work in us.

Let's get started with "The Principalities and Powers."

Introduction To The Powers

The principalities and powers are fallen angels that were given authority to rule over the nations that were exiled at Babel due to disobedience and scattered across the face of the earth. As Moses put it:

> *When the Most High apportioned the nations, when he divided humankind, he fixed the boundaries of the peoples according to the number of the gods; the Lord's own portion was his people, Jacob his allotted share. (Deuteronomy 32:8–9, NRSV)*

As is clear here, the fallen angels became the false "gods" (*elohim*) of the nations.

However, the powers have a bit of history that precedes Babel. (For a full treatment of the powers, read *Unseen Realm* by Michael Heisser.)

First of all, angels were created to be servants (*diakonos*) to humans. As Hebrews puts it:

> *Are not all angels spirits in the divine service, sent to serve for the sake of those who are to inherit salvation? (Hebrews 1:14, NRSV)*

Paul tells us in Colossians 1 that the powers were first created by Jesus to administrate the cosmos in partnership with humans.

> *He is the image of the invisible God, the firstborn of all creation; for in him all things in heaven and on earth were created, things visible and invisible, whether thrones or dominions or rulers or powers —all things have been created through him and for him. He himself is before all things, and in him all things hold together. (Colossians 1:15–17, NRSV)*

The phrase, "thrones or dominions or rulers or powers," is rendered "thrones, dominions, principalities or powers" in the traditional King James Version. In Paul's thought, the same "principalities and powers" that became the fallen powers that dominated the nations were originally created by Jesus to assist human dominion.

However, some of the angels rebelled (apparently led by the figure we have come to know as "Satan," or "the devil") against this assignment and revolted against God. Contrary to popular Christian mythology, the Bible does not teach that Satan rebelled against God prior to the creation of humans. Rather, Scripture implies that Satan and his angels rebelled in the Garden of Eden.

(The famous passages in Isaiah 14, Ezekiel 28 and Revelation 12 do not describe a pre-cosmic fall of Satan. Again, to learn more about this, read *Unseen Realm* by Michael Heisser.)

After Satan's fall in Eden, there seems to be another rebellion in Genesis 6, where "the sons of God" took wives of "the daughters of men" and became tyrants over the earth. Their offspring became an angel-human hybrid race of giants called "the Nephilim." The corruption of the human race and of the earth was so pervasive that God sent the flood to wipe out the hybrid seed and preserve Noah (who alone was pure in his lineage) and his family.

The fallen angels who had mingled with humans were imprisoned in Tartarus (2 Peter 2:4), and their Nephilim offspring were disembodied, which Jewish tradition points to as the origin of demons. Genesis 6 also tells us that there were further "irruptions" of angels interbreeding with humans and producing giants, but never again did they succeed in taking over the earth. The conquest of Canaan by Israel was a divine assignment to eradicate the giants once for all. As far as we can tell, David finally finished the task.

This brings us back to Babel, where the humans under the leadership of Nimrod refused to obey God's command to Noah to be fruitful and multiply and fill up the earth, just as God had commanded Adam. At Babel, God divided their languages and scattered them across the face of the earth.

God then gave the seventy Gentile nations over to another group of fallen angels in order to prevent them from uniting again as they had done at Babel and once again fully corrupting the earth. As Paul put it when referring to Israel's exile, God "shut them up"—literally, imprisoned them—in unbelief that he might work out his redemptive purpose, which he did through Abraham, Isaac and Israel. Babel was the exile of the Gentile nations.

Though the powers were fallen angels, they still had access to the "Divine Council" (which we will discuss further below) and were often summoned before the Most High to give an account of their rule over humans.

You may remember the example in Job where Satan came to present himself before God with all the other Sons of God, but Psalm 82 is the most explicit example of the powers in the Divine Council. It is worth reading in full:

1 God has taken his place in the divine council; in the midst of the gods he holds judgment:

2 "How long will you judge unjustly and show partiality to the wicked? Selah 3 Give justice to the weak and the orphan; maintain the right of the lowly and the destitute. 4 Rescue the weak and the needy; deliver them from the hand of the wicked." 5 They have neither knowledge nor understanding, they walk around in darkness; all the foundations of the earth are shaken.

6 I say, "You are gods, children of the Most High, all of you; 7 nevertheless, you shall die like mortals, and fall like any prince."

8 Rise up, O God, judge the earth; for all the nations belong to you! (Psalm 82:1–8, NRSV)

The powers are described most fully in Daniel. In Daniel (and elsewhere), the powers are called "princes," the princes of the nations. In Daniel and Ezekiel, we read about the Prince of Babylon, the Prince of Persia, the Prince of Greece, the Prince of Tyre, the Prince of Sidon, and Michael, the Prince of

Israel. These are the ones who are named, but there were certainly many others, the princes of nations that masqueraded as gods within pagan pantheons.

These are the shadowy figures that emerge blinking in the full light of the New Testament as "the rulers...the authorities...the cosmic powers of this present darkness...the spiritual forces of evil in the heavenly places" (Ephesians 6:12, NRSV). Paul refers to them in Ephesians 1, 3, 6; Colossians 1, 2; Romans 8; 1 Corinthians 15; and Peter mentions them in 1 Peter 3. These passages and others describe a reality simply taken for granted by New Testament writers, the dark reality of a cadre of fallen angels that dominated the earth.

These are the figures that Paul describes as working through "the *stoicheia*," the "spirit systems" of the world. (Colossians 2) And they are the despotic tyrants of the nations that Jesus came to expose and expel. As we shall see, much of Paul's kingdom theology is given to explain how Jesus recovered the authority that had been given to the powers and how God the Father, through Jesus and his Spirit-filled ekklesia, is subduing those deposed powers under Christ's feet. (1 Corinthians 15)

Let's go to Unit 5 and discuss how Jesus triumphed over the powers.

UNIT 5: MATTHEW 28: THE GREAT COMMISSION

And Jesus came and said to them, "All authority in heaven and on earth has been given to me."

"Go therefore and make disciples of all nations, baptizing them in the name of the Father and of the Son and of the Holy Spirit, and teaching them to obey everything that I have commanded you."

"And remember, I am with you always, to the end of the age." (Matthew 28:18–20, NRSV)

All Authority In Heaven and On Earth

In order to truly understand the kingdom, we must get a better grasp on what Jesus meant when he declared that he had received "all authority in heaven and on earth." In order to get that better grasp, we must talk a bit more about angels.

As we saw above, the angels were created to serve the heirs of salvation, to assist humans in the work of cosmic dominion. Some of the angels rebelled against this assignment and became fallen angels, "the powers" we discussed above.

The fallen angels (led by the dark figure we call "Satan") rebelled against their assignment in Eden and in Genesis 6. Many of these angels cohabited with human females, propagating the Nephilim, and were cast into the abyss until the last judgment to restrain their evil actions.

At Babel, other fallen angels were given domination over the seventy nations of the earth, when God gave the nations over to serve false gods (as they desired to do). (Deuteronomy 32:8. Cf. Acts 7:42 and Romans 1:24, 26, 28 for examples of God giving people up to their own desires in order to chasten their hearts and bring them to repentance.) This gave angels delegated administration over the seventy nations, an administration that they did not manage well (as we saw in Psalm 82).

God called Abraham out of the scattered nations and made a covenant with him that his offspring would be God's chosen nation. After 400 years of sojourn in Canaan and Egypt, Israel was led out of Egypt in the Exodus to inherit the land God had promised to Abraham.

Then, at Sinai, Israel rejected God's divine invitation to commune with him face-to-face and learn his law through love. (Deuteronomy 5:27) They chose rather to receive the law "ordained through angels by a mediator" (Galatians 3:19, NRSV). This brings us to a little-known fact: the law of Moses was given through the "rankings" ("disposition" in the KJV) of angels. (Acts 7:53) As Hebrews puts it, the law of Moses was "declared through angels"

(Hebrews 2:2). This was the beginning of "middle-man religion" in Israel.

(This is why Paul describes the attempt to syncretize the Mosaic religion within the Christian faith as "the worship of angels." [Colossians 2:18] When we observe rules rather than relationship, we end up embracing the "thing" instead of the Father. This is what Jesus taught when he asked, "Which is greater, the sabbath or the Lord of the sabbath? Which is more important, the sabbath or man? Is man for sabbath or sabbath for man?" On and on.)

Moses and the angels collaborated on the law, but neither Moses nor the angels saw the complete picture of God the Father revealed in Jesus. Moses desired to see the full glory of God, but was allowed only to see the "hinder parts" of God, the "lesser glory." The angels longed to look into the full mystery of God's purpose manifest in Christ, but were unable to see it clearly. (1 Peter 1:12) This is why John declared:

> *The law indeed was given through Moses; grace and truth came through Jesus Christ.* **No one has ever seen God.** *It is God the only Son, who is close to the Father's heart, who has made him known. (John 1:17–18, NRSV).*

Jesus came to reveal the Father and make him known. Because of the flesh, the law could only approximate at best—and distort at worst—what God was like. This is why much of Jesus's teaching clarified God's true heart and "fulfilled the law and the prophets."

The Old Covenant era was the age of angels. The seventy nations of the earth were under the domination of fallen angels. Israel was under the mediated administration of Moses and the angels. Then, Israel turned away repeatedly to idols, and God finally gave them up to serve the false gods they lusted after. As Stephen put it, "But God turned away from them and handed them over to worship the host of heaven" (Acts 7:42, NRSV). The *shekinah* glory of God departed from the temple in Jerusalem, and God handed Israel over the principalities and powers, the princes of the Gentile nations.

This was called "the Exile." And this takes us back to Daniel 9 where God extended Israel's exile to 490 years. Israel, as Daniel saw so clearly in his dreams and visions, would remain under the power of world empires (the lion, bear, leopard and terrible beast) until the time of Messiah.

When Jesus came, both Israel and the nations were under the heel of the powers. Jerusalem and Rome were locked in corrupt collusion, and the Father's House, the temple, had been made into a "den of thieves," as Jesus put it. This is why Paul so boldly (and scandalously!) described both Judaism and paganism as "the elements of the world," the *"stoicheia,"* the "spirit-systems" of the world. (Galatians 4:3, 9; Colossians 2:8) Paul saw the *stoicheia* as the institutional spirit-systems of both Jerusalem and Rome that had become "the habitation of devils" (Revelation 18:2).

This is why Jesus and the apostles spent so much time discussing "the coming of the Lord" in judgment upon Jerusalem, when the temple would be destroyed and the old stoicheia of corrupt Judaism would be cast into hell—which would also signal the beginning of the end of world empires. The stoicheia would be overthrown and the reign of King Jesus established in every nation under heaven.

All this (and much more!) is why Jesus said that he had been given "all authority in heaven and on earth." The Creator of all things—the one who created "all things in heaven and on earth…things visible and invisible, whether thrones or dominions or rulers or powers" at the beginning—had come to earth as the divine-human Son of God to reclaim all authority in heaven and on earth *on behalf of his human brothers and sisters*. (Hebrews 2:17)

Every realm of angelic and human dominion was restored to Christ who instituted all authority in the beginning. But now, the authority was given to Jesus as a glorified *human*, and not just as the eternal Son of God, the Creator. And as a *human*, Jesus restored humans to their predestined glory, seated with him in the heavens ruling and reigning forever.

When Jesus ascended into heaven, he was presented before the Father as the faithful Son, the one who "learned obedience through what he suffered" (Hebrews 5:8, NRSV). Although he was a Son, in his obedience, Christ overturned the disobedience of humans and was thus recognized as the faithful Son and heir of all creation.

Jesus then received all authority in heaven and earth as an ascended and exalted *human*. Jesus' victory over sin and death was accomplished as a *man*, not only as God (though he never ceased to be God, for sure). Jesus' ascent into heaven was a fulfillment of the original destiny of humans to be glorified and drawn into union with the triune God. Jesus accomplished what Adam failed to accomplish.

The Head of the Nations

Paul stated that Christ was raised from the dead and ascended into heaven to be the head of all nations.

> *God put this power to work in Christ when he raised him from the dead and seated him at his right hand in the heavenly places, far above all rule and authority and power and dominion, and above every name that is named, not only in this age but also in the age to come. And he has put all things under his feet and has made him the head over all things for the church, which is his body, the fullness of him who fills all in all. (Ephesians 1:20–23, NRSV)*

When Christ ascended, God the Father gave him the authority of all angels in heaven and all humans on earth. The principalities and powers that had dominated the nations were dethroned and stripped of their power. Satan and the powers, who rightly claimed that they had been given the kingdoms of the earth (Luke 4:5-7), were expelled from their heavenly *oikonomia* and replaced by the ascended King.

As Paul put it in Colossians:

He disarmed (stripped) the rulers and authorities and made a public example of them, triumphing over them in it. (Colossians 2:15, NRSV)

Peter declared that Jesus "has gone into heaven and is at the right hand of God, with angels, authorities, and powers made subject to him" (1 Peter 3:22, NRSV).

The age of angels was over, and the age of sons and daughters had begun. The nations had been promised to Jesus:

"Ask of me, and I will make the nations your heritage, and the ends of the earth your possession" (Psalm 2:8, NRSV).

The Father was now keeping that promise. When Jesus ascended, he was given title deed to the nations. Through death, Christ shattered the power of the evil ones, the ancient gods who ruled through fear. Through death, Jesus destroyed the one who had the power of death, that is, the devil, and he freed those who all their lives were held in slavery by the fear of death. (Hebrews 2:14–15, NRSV)

Through his resurrection and ascension, Jesus became the head—the originator, the founder—of a new humanity now seated with him in heavenly places. Through his ascension, Jesus became the head of the nations. The nations were his inheritance, and since they now belonged to him, he commissioned us to go and actualize that reality.

Thus the Great Commission.

Disciple the Nations

In the Great Commission, Jesus commanded us—in light of his universal, cosmic authority—to "disciple the nations." Not just, "make disciples from within the nations," but actually *disciple the nations*.

The nations belong to Jesus. They are his rightful inheritance. We are heralds of that good news (*euangelion*). And we are *effectuators* of that good news. By heralding the good news and baptizing those who believe it into the new humanity of Christ that draws us into the triune life of God, we release the kingdom of God into the world.

The powers have been dethroned and the nations have been given to Christ. But that reality must be realized. And we are the means through which that reality is realized. *Changed people change the world.*

The Conquest of the Nations

The powers do not readily accept their fate. The ascension of Jesus and his accession to the throne of God expelled the fallen powers from the Divine Council and cast them down to the earth. (Revelation 12) As Jesus put it, "Now is the judgment of this world; now the ruler of this world will be driven out" (John 12:31, NRSV).

Some mistakenly believe that Satan and his angels still have access to the Courts of Heaven, but they do not. The "accuser of the brethren" has been replaced by the Advocate. The only courtroom Satan has access to now is the courtroom of your mind, if you give audience to his lies. The powers have no access to heaven, to the Divine Council.

You and I have taken their place.

But the powers fight desperately to retain their domination over the earth. The powers become entrenched within human social systems, within religion, politics, government, education, technology, media, medicine, business, economies, universities, shopping malls—anywhere humans gather and offer opportunities for spiritual influence. These spirit-systems are the stoicheia.

When believers come preaching the good news of Christ's enthronement, the powers dig in. They fight back with ferocious intensity. This is spiritual warfare, and it is real. Never underestimate the fury of a displaced principality. They will fight like hell—literally.

The most oft-quoted Old Testament passage in the New Testament, Psalm 110, says, "The Lord says to my lord, 'Sit at my right hand until I make your enemies your footstool.'" (Psalm 110:1, NRSV). Jesus was seated at the right hand of the Father when he ascended, and the enemies that are being made his footstool are the powers.

Paul quoted Psalm 110 in 1 Corinthians 15:

Then comes the end, when he hands over the kingdom to God the Father, after he has destroyed every ruler and every authority and power. For he must reign until he has put all his enemies under his feet. The last enemy to be destroyed is death. (1 Corinthians 15:24–26, NRSV)

Hebrews quotes it:

But when Christ had offered for all time a single sacrifice for sins, "he sat down at the right hand of God," and since then has been waiting "until his enemies would be made a footstool for his feet." (Hebrews 10:12–13, NRSV)

God the Father is subduing Christ's enemies under his feet through the collaborative effort of the Holy Spirit in the ekklesia. We bind on earth what has been bound in heaven. We'll talk more about the work of the Spirit through the ekklesia below, but for now we must simply highlight our cooperative effort in the Great Commission.

We are co-heirs and co-laborers with Christ. Through the power of the Holy Spirit within us, we advance into every nation binding the powers and bringing the stoicheia into alignment with Christ. As Paul put it:

With all wisdom and insight he has made known to us the mystery of his will, according to his good pleasure that he set forth in Christ, as a plan for the fullness of time, to gather up all things in him, things in heaven and things on earth. (Ephesians 1:8–10, NRSV)

God has a plan to "gather up"—literally, "to align under one head"—everything in heaven and earth, every realm of angels and humans, in Christ. And we are assigned the task of witnessing that reality to the ends of the earth. (Acts 1:8) And Jesus promised he would be with us "always, even to the end of the age" (Matthew 28:18–20, NRSV).

UNIT 6: EPHESIANS 3: THE REPATRIATION OF THE NATIONS

The earth is the Lord's and all that is in it, the world, and those who live in it. (Psalm 24:1, NRSV)

Ask of me, and I will make the nations your heritage, and the ends of the earth your possession. (Psalm 2:8, NRSV)

For this reason I bow my knees before the Father, from whom every family in heaven and on earth takes its name. (Ephesians 3:14–15, NRSV)

The nations belong to Jesus. But they, like the prodigal son, departed from the Father's house and wasted their inheritance in a far away land. But Christ, embodying the human race, returned to the Father on our behalf, opening the way for the reconciliation of all nations to God.

As the representative Son, the eternal Christ was "adopted" by the Father into full human sonship, with all the rights and privileges, "and was declared to be Son of God with power according to the spirit of holiness by resurrection from the dead" (Romans 1:4, NRSV). In Christ, the nations have returned home.

Of course, all of that must be worked out in real time in the real world, which is what the ekklesia has been doing since Pentecost. Reconciliation is a finished work, but now the reconciled must *be* reconciled. Thus, we have been given "the ministry" and "the word" of reconciliation. (2 Corinthians 5:18-19)

At Babel, human languages were divided and the nations were scattered. At Pentecost, the tongues were united (in message) and the nations were gathered. The Great Commission launched a universal "end of exile" announcement project, where believers are empowered by the Holy Spirit to be witnesses of Christ "in Jerusalem, Judaea, Samaria, unto the ends of the earth" (Acts 1:8), fulfilling the promise of Psalm 2:

> *Ask of me, and I will make the nations your heritage, and the ends of the earth your possession. (Psalm 2:8, NRSV)*

Kingdom Repatriation

The return of the nations to the Father is kingdom repatriation. The idea of kingdom repatriation comes from Ephesians 3.

> *For this reason I bow my knees before the Father (pater), from whom every family (patria) in heaven and on earth takes its name. (Ephesians 3:14–15, NRSV)*

We are wrestling with the powers, Paul says, as we advance the transformation of the kingdom in the world. (Ephesians 6:12) They do not want to submit to the rule of Christ, but we come preaching the good news that all nations have been liberated from slavery to the false gods of the world and are now free to serve their true Lord. This displaces and subdues the powers in every nation, in every city, family and tribe. That is what we reveal to the powers as we display the manifold wisdom of God.

So that through the church the wisdom of God in its rich variety might now be made known to the rulers and authorities in the heavenly places. (Ephesians 3:10, NRSV)

Through baptism, the ekklesia officiates the "re-fathering" and consequent "re-naming" of the families of the earth. The seventy nations of Genesis 10 all received their names from their earthly fathers, their tribal identity, and they were all exiled and excluded from the family of God, even though God still owned all the nations.

11 So then, remember that at one time you Gentiles by birth, called "the uncircumcision" by those who are called "the circumcision"—a physical circumcision made in the flesh by human hands—12 remember that you were at that time without Christ, being aliens from the commonwealth of Israel, and strangers to the covenants of promise, having no hope and without God in the world.

13 But now in Christ Jesus you who once were far off have been brought near by the blood of Christ. 14 For he is our peace; in his flesh he has made both groups into one and has broken down the dividing wall, that is, the hostility between us.

15 He has abolished the law with its commandments and ordinances, that he might create in himself one new humanity in place of the two, thus making peace, 16 and might reconcile both groups to God in one body through the cross, thus putting to death that hostility through it.

17 So he came and proclaimed peace to you who were far off and peace to those who were near; 18 for through him both of us have access in one Spirit to the Father.

19 So then you are no longer strangers and aliens, but you are citizens with the saints and also members of the household of God, 20 built upon the foundation of the apostles and prophets, with Christ Jesus himself as the cornerstone.

21 In him the whole structure is joined together and grows into a holy temple in the Lord; 22 in whom you also are built together spiritually into a dwelling place for God. (Ephesians 2:11–22, NRSV)

From Babel onward, the powers fragmented the nations and dominated them through tribal identity and political division—divide and conquer. The powers cultivated hostility, as Paul mentioned above, and branded the nations, reshaping them in their diabolical image. But when Christ received "by inheritance" the name that is "above every name that is named," the renaming and re-fathering of the nations was underway. The divided nations were reunited in Christ, which is enacted in the earth through baptism by the ekklesia.

> *As many of you as were **baptized** into Christ have clothed yourselves with Christ. There is no longer Jew or Greek, there is no longer slave or free, there is no longer male and female; **for all of you are one in Christ Jesus**. And if you belong to Christ, then you are Abraham's offspring, heirs according to the promise. (Galatians 3:27–29, NRSV)*

Baptism lies at the center of this "refamiliation" of the nations. Through baptism, believers take on the name of the Lord as they invoke his name in their faith-confession. They take on his name and receive a new personal name, as Jesus promised. This refamiliation is the basis for re-identification in every nation. The orphaned nations are restored like prodigals back to the eagerly awaiting Father.

The local, regional, national and global ekklesia participates in this re-identification of the nations.

Just as Mansfield has been called after Ralph Man and Julian Feild, so it is now being re-named as "God's field." The renaming of a region releases the true identity of that region in Christ.

(Another example of kingdom repatriation is the Order of Melchizedek with its refathering and refamiliation of temple worship through Melchizedek's eternal order. The priesthood of Levi was from the earthly, fleshly order of "men that die." But the Order of Melchizedek is an eternal order, one not rooted in earthly genealogies. The Order of Melchizedek is the basis for "the universal priesthood of believers," for we are not priests based on earthly genealogy.)

This refamiliation of the nations starts with the individual believer but then moves into the household. That's what Paul emphasized in Ephesians 5, the transformed person becomes a transformed family, and transformed families become transformed cities and nations. Cultures shift through the work of the ekklesia.

The repatriation of the heart is absolutely essential to the repatriation of the nations. The repatriation of the heart is the process by which we redeem our human bloodlines and bring our genealogy and genetics under the bloodline of Jesus. We do not forsake our earthly heritage, but we honor our father and mother by representational repentance for our ancestry, by forgiving our forefathers and mothers for the sins they committed. We redeem our family line by bringing it under the renaming hand of Abba Father. This is all a part of our adoption.

The refathering, refamiliation and repatriation of the nations is all rooted in Christ's true revelation of the Father. All sin and death in the world came from the lie humans first believed in the Garden about God. The law and the prophets perpetuated much misunderstanding about the Father through "middleman religion." Jesus came to tell the truth about the Father and heal the self-inflicted Father wounds that broke the human spirit.

Repatriating Angels

Another fascinating idea is the possibility of repatriating angels. Paul says that "all families in heaven and on earth" (same phrasing as the Great Commission) receive their name from the Father. This surely refers to all the ranks of holy angels being brought under the authority of Jesus in his ascension.

But could this also include the repatriation of the fallen angels? Can fallen angels repent and serve the purpose of Christ? It is certainly true in Daniel 7 that some of the beasts (world governments) were cast into hell, while others were kept alive and ruled by the Son of Man.

For example, can the spirit of mammon in Mansfield be brought under the dominion of King Jesus and made to serve "the heirs of salvation."[11]

Can a local/regional spirit of mammon be repatriated and renamed so that it serves King Jesus?

No doubt, holy angels are "renamed" under the lordship of Jesus. They are "rebranded" as servants of the Son of God, of the redeemed human race. They serve under his banner. But what about the powers?

As we shall discuss further below, the ekklesia releases the keys of the kingdom of heaven, and individual believers carry those keys out into their "assigned area of influence," their "metron." (2 Corinthians 10:12-16) The keys of the kingdom are words of life that open the gates of death. Everywhere that death has reigned, we are authorized to release life and life more abundantly. Death manifests as the works of the flesh, and the keys of life open the gates and deliver the captives.

My question is this: when we are given keys of the kingdom to a particular field, does the principality of that metron come under our dominion and serve our interests? In other words, can we require the spirit of mammon in Mansfield to switch sides? Can we require, with the authority we have been given—through the name we have inherited—that the spirit of mammon start working with the ekklesia to release prosperity to all and expel "the old spirit of injustice" that has characterized Mansfield?

Did Daniel do this with Nebuchadnezzar? Was Daniel's "harnessing" of the kings of Babylon and Persia an example of principalities that are restrained and required to serve? Another example would be Joseph with Pharaoh. It could be possible that we must learn to discern which powers can be harnessed and which ones must be banished to the abyss.

We need to discuss this further.

Sheep and Goat Nations

This brings us to the judgment and separation of the nations Jesus spoke about in Matthew 25. Most Christians have been trained to see Matthew 25 as the last judgment at the end of history, but in reality Matthew 25 is a continuation of Matthew 24, where Jesus prophesied the destruction of Jerusalem. The judgment scene in Matthew 25 is a direct allusion to Daniel 7 and the ongoing judgment of the nations.

> *As I watched in the night visions, I saw one like a human being coming with the clouds of heaven. And* ***he came to the Ancient One and was presented before him***. *To him was given dominion and glory and kingship, that all peoples, nations, and languages should serve him. His dominion is an everlasting dominion that shall not pass away, and his kingship is one that shall never be destroyed. (Daniel 7:13–14, NRSV)*
>
> *Then the court shall sit in judgment, and his dominion shall be taken away, to be consumed and totally destroyed. The kingship and dominion and the greatness of the kingdoms under the*

> *whole heaven shall be given to the people of the holy ones of the Most High; their kingdom shall be an everlasting kingdom, and all dominions shall serve and obey them." (Daniel 7:26–27, NRSV)*

It is important to note that this judgment happens when the Son of Man ascends *up to* the Ancient of Days. This judgment happens after Christ's ascension and enthronement in the heavenly courts, in the Divine Council. And Jesus echoes this:

> *When the Son of Man comes in his glory, and all the angels with him, then he will sit on the throne of his glory. All the nations will be gathered before him, and he will separate people [them] one from another as a shepherd separates the sheep from the goats, and he will put the sheep at his right hand and the goats at the left. (Matthew 25:31–33, NRSV)*

As Daniel 7:27 makes clear, the judgment of the nations happens in collaboration with "the saints of the Most High." The ekklesia administers the judgment of the nations as we fulfill the Great Commission. As Jesus told us, the nations will be judged for their response to our kingdom witness, our *euangelion*. Though there will certainly be a "Last Judgment," the judgment of the nations was inaugurated in AD 70 and has continued since.

Jesus is seated on his throne of glory, having ascended up to the Ancient of Days. We are seated with him, and we are confronting the powers with a choice: "Kiss the Son! Or lose your position." (Psalm 2:10-11) If they kiss the Son and submit to the rule of Christ, then possibly their angelic power may be redeemed and their energy redirected toward the kingdom of God. They may be repatriated back to their original purpose of serving the heirs of salvation, rather than dominating and exploiting them.

If they do not kiss the Son, then we are authorized to vacate their rule and evict them from their position. They are then cast into hell just like Jesus cast demons into the abyss. The "eternal fire" that the goat nations are cast into in Matthew 25 is the same fire that the beasts are cast into in Daniel 7.

> *I watched then because of the noise of the arrogant words that the horn was speaking. And as I watched, the beast was put to death, and its body destroyed and given over to be burned with fire. (Daniel 7:11, NRSV)*

> *Then he will say to those at his left hand, "You that are accursed, depart from me into the eternal fire prepared for the devil and his angels." (Matthew 25:41, NRSV)*

The parallels are significant.

Why Does It Matter?

It matters simply because we cannot understand the full scope of our assignment if we do not grasp what's happening in heaven and on earth. If we hope to fulfill the Great Commission, then we must understand Christ's authority in heaven and on earth.

We must also understand how the nations are being repatriated as Christ's full inheritance. And we must understand how all this is happening *now*, prior to the Second Coming. As we shall see below, *we must not postpone the kingdom until after Christ returns*. The entire reason for his ascension was to omnipresence his Spirit in believers and multiply exponentially the rule of Christ from the heavens into the earth.

Most importantly, it matters because Jesus will not return until the work is complete, until his enemies are subdued and the kingdom has come in every nation. As Peter said, Jesus "must remain in heaven until the time of universal restoration that God announced long ago through his holy prophets" (Acts 3:21, NRSV). Ironically, Christians who embrace escapist eschatology and pray for a divine evacuation are delaying Christ's return by refusing to partner with the Spirit in fulfilling the Great Commission.

We must pray more than ever, "Let your kingdom come."

MODULE 3: HOW THE KINGDOM COMES IN THE WORLD

UNIT 7: PERSONAL & FAMILY TRANSFORMATION

The kingdom comes spiritually, gradually and fully. The kingdom takes root in the Spirit-filled human heart and flows out of our fingertips into the world around us. *Changed people change the world.*

The Spirit opens up a well in our "belly," the deepest region of our being. The Spirit fills our human spirit and then flows up through our soul, initiating change in our emotions, will and mind. How we feel, how we decide and how we think are radically recalibrated as we are filled with the Spirit.

Our thought-life is transformed. (Check out *The Supernatural Power of A Transformed Mind* by Bill Johnson for a powerful understanding of how our mind is changed by the mind of Christ.)

Then, our speech begins to change—which is incredibly important. Our words create our world, so learning to say only what we hear the Father say is a big deal. Most Christians sabotage their dominion simply by partnering with the enemy's lies through the words they speak.

(Also check out *Keywords* by Steve Pixler to learn how the words you speak become keys that open the gates of hell and give you dominion in your world.)

Finally, our actions and behavior start manifesting externally the change we experience internally. We begin to manifest the kingdom. Our Spirit-filled thoughts, words and deeds become the portal through which heaven breaks into earth.

This is how the kingdom comes.

Inner Healing

Personal transformation requires inner healing. The will to change can only take us so far unless we are willing to face the profoundly uncomfortable process of being healed in our soul and body. In Christ, our human spirit is made new all at once, totally and completely. *It is is done!* But what is done must *be* done through the process of retraining our emotions, will and mind. This is inner healing.

Inner healing confronts the lies we have believed (usually through trauma) about God, self and others. Satan has no power except the power of a lie, which is why he is the "father of lies" and a murderer from the beginning. He is a serial killer who ensnares, enslaves and exterminates his victims through lies.

Deliverance

Inner healing often requires deliverance. Deliverance is when we confront the demons that have infested our soul and body through the lies that gave them access. Deliverance is more than rooting out a lie from our childhood. Deliverance is actually confronting real demons and commanding them to leave. People often become demonized when they submit to dehumanizing behaviors that enslave their soul and body. But Jesus gave believers authority and power to expel demons. This is huge part of how the kingdom comes.

(Read Kris Vallotton, *Spirit Wars* for a powerful look at deliverance and spiritual warfare.)

When our soul and body are healed, when demons are expelled, we begin to re-groove the neural pathways of our brain and reconstitute the molecular makeup of our bodies. We physically manifest the change happening on the inside. This is what Paul calls the "sanctification of spirit, soul and body" (1 Thessalonians 5:23; see also 2 Corinthians 7:1.)

Generational Healing

As we are healed, we will come to understand that every human exists within a "stream" of being that flows from the past and into the future. We are connected—whether we know it or not—to our ancestors and descendants. We inherit the genealogical legacy of our ancestors, and we help shape the future our generations will enjoy.

This means that much of our personal healing will trace back to "generational iniquity" that took root in our fathers and mothers and was passed down through our genes and through the epigenetic markers that our DNA carries. This is the "sins of the fathers" that Scripture talks so much about.

To be clear, we are not judged and held guilty for anything anyone else has ever done. Generational iniquity is not about being punished for someone else's crime. Jesus took the curse upon him at the cross and every generational curse was broken in him. Yet what *was* broken must *be* broken. In other words, we must apply through faith what Christ has done.

Representational Repentance

Representational repentance is a tool that Moses and Daniel (and others) used in Scripture to stand in for a group of people and repent on their behalf. Though it does not expiate the sins of individual people—if it did, we would stand right now and repent on behalf of the entire human race!—representational repentance does break the power of corporate sins.

The repentance of an individual may not heal every member of a family, for example, but it can break family strongholds and bring deliverance to the one who is willing to turn from lies to truth.

Generational Momentum

The kingdom of God comes gradually. Indeed, the kingdom of God comes *generationally*. The deliberate strategy of God since creation has been to grow his purpose in the earth through generational momentum.

When God first gave humans the dominion mandate in Eden, he told them:

"Be fruitful and multiply, and fill the earth and subdue it; and have dominion over the fish of the sea and over the birds of the air and over every living thing that moves upon the earth." (Genesis 1:28, NRSV)

Human dominion was directly tied to human propagation. In the New Covenant, Christians tend to spiritualize this mandate and see fruitfulness and multiplication only as evangelism. However, a quick look through the New Testament shows that the early church still saw a link between the advance of the kingdom and the covenant household. For example, take a quick look at the passages where entire households were saved. The emphasis on leading whole families to Christ is significant.

One of the clearest statements of the generational aspect of kingdom advance is Acts 2:39:

For the promise is for you, for your children, and for all who are far away, everyone whom the Lord our God calls to him. (Acts 2:39, NRSV)

The promise of the Holy Spirit is to *you*, to *your children*, and then to those far away. This is an incredible scripture. Peter does not hesitate to declare that our children are children of promise. We can expect that God will be faithful to save our kids. And through their salvation, the Holy Spirit will launch generational momentum that will grow in the earth.

As God assured Abraham, blessings accrue to each subsequent generation. We often focus on the negative aspects of "generational curses," but Abraham's story highlights the power of *generational blessings*. The blessings grow exponentially throughout the generations.

And that is God's kingdom strategy. The kingdom comes *gradually*. The kingdom comes *generationally*.

In order for the kingdom to advance in the world, believers must exercise audacious faith regarding their generations. Our generations are not secure because we are faithful—they are secure because God is faithful. Certainly, he works out that faithfulness in us, but his promise is a promise of grace, not works. We must *believe* that our kids are promise kids simply because God made the promise—not because we have earned it.

The enemy has undermined our generational faith for generations simply by sucking the air out of our faith through shame. We perform poorly as parents, and then come into agreement with the lie that the salvation and shalom of our children is dependent on our performance. No. No, it's not. The salvation of our generations is exactly like the salvation of our souls:

> *For by grace you have been saved through faith, and this is not your own doing; it is the gift of God—not the result of works, so that no one may boast. (Ephesians 2:8–9, NRSV)*

It is time to believe God's promise regarding our children. Our perfectionism isn't working. Let's try faith.

The Synergy Between the Kingdom and the *Oikos*

As we saw above, the repatriation of the nations begins with the repatriation of the human heart as we return to the Father. Then, repatriation flows into the household and, finally, out to the nations.

The household is a key component to kingdom repatriation. The ekklesia is the "household" and "family" of God. Paul uses this idea repeatedly. The temple is the Father's house, and the ekklesia is his cosmic temple, his universal family in heaven and earth.

In Ephesians, Paul makes explicit the direct connection between the household of faith and the Christian family. It is no accident that he weaves together the transformation of the pagan world (Ephesians 4:17-5:20) and the reframing of the Christian household (Ephesians 5:21-6:9). Paul then—again, no accident!—wraps it all up with the powerful, famous section on spiritual warfare:

Finally, be strong in the Lord and in the strength of his power. Put on the whole armor of God, so that you may be able to stand against the wiles of the devil. For our struggle is not against enemies of blood and flesh, but against the rulers, against the authorities, against the cosmic powers of this present darkness, against the spiritual forces of evil in the heavenly places.

Therefore take up the whole armor of God, so that you may be able to withstand on that evil day, and having done everything, to stand firm. (Ephesians 6:10–13, NRSV)

Building the household of God, the "habitation of God through the Spirit," and rebuilding families is directly linked to the war going on in the heavens and on the earth. The principalities and powers, the rulers of the darkness of this world and spiritual wickedness in high places are fighting ruthlessly to destroy the human family. Why? Because the kingdom is directly linked to generational momentum, and if the enemy can fracture and pervert the family, the covenant household, then he can frustrate the advance of Christ's kingdom.

Paul uses several "house" words to describe the work of the kingdom. Here's a few:

1. *Oikos* — house
2. *Oikonomos* — steward of the house

3. *Oikonomia* — administration of the house (think plan or budget)

4. *Oikumene* — the world (society)

5. *Oikodome* — building (edifying) the house

In Ephesians, Paul traces an intrinsic connection between the household of God and refathered families. The transformation of society must take root in the *oikos*. That then flows out through the leadership of the *oikonomos* to the *oikonomia*, the "house-administration." (The way business is done.) The *oikonomia* then reshapes the *oikumene*, the world system, human society. This may be the closest to our modern idea of "culture" we can find in the New Testament.

Did you trace the continuum? The kingdom comes in the individual; then in the family; and, finally, in the world.

In Ephesians 5, Paul demonstrates how the kingdom subverts and overthrows twisted human culture when he alluded to the Aristotelian "household codes" in his instruction to Christian families. Paul used the framework of the household codes, but embedded kingdom liberation and transformation within them when he taught everyone to submit to each other; for wives to submit "as to the Lord"; for husbands to love their wives as Christ loved the church; for masters and slaves to serve each other as if they were serving Christ.

Paul released the apostolic transformation of society through the subversive transformation of the ancient households. "There is no longer Jew or Greek, there is no longer slave or free, there is no longer male and female; for all of you are one in Christ Jesus" (Galatians 3:28). Paul understood very well that this was the radical reorganization of the cosmos in Christ. The walls of hostility are broken down.

When the nations are repatriated to the Father, the promise to Abraham is fulfilled:

> *3 Then Abram fell on his face; and God said to him, 4 "As for me, this is my covenant with you: You shall be the ancestor of a multitude of nations. 5 No longer shall your name be Abram, but your name shall be Abraham; for I have made you the ancestor of a multitude of nations. 6 I will make you exceedingly fruitful; and I will make nations of you, and kings shall come from you."*
>
> *7 "I will establish my covenant between me and you, and your offspring after you throughout their generations, for an everlasting covenant, to be God to you and to your offspring after you. 8 And I will give to you, and to your offspring after you, the land where you are now an alien, all the land of Canaan, for a perpetual holding; and I will be their God." (Genesis 17:3–8, NRSV)*

As Paul put it, this was "the gospel preached first to Abraham" (Galatians 3:8). The gospel of the kingdom is intrinsically bound up with the blessing of all nations. We must settle for nothing less.

UNIT 8: EKKLESIA

Now when Jesus came into the district of Caesarea Philippi, he asked his disciples, "Who do people say that the Son of Man is?" And they said, "Some say John the Baptist, but others Elijah, and still others Jeremiah or one of the prophets."

He said to them, "But who do you say that I am?" Simon Peter answered, "You are the Messiah, the Son of the living God."

And Jesus answered him, "Blessed are you, Simon son of Jonah! For flesh and blood has not revealed this to you, but my Father in heaven. And I tell you, you are Peter, and on this rock I will build my church, and the gates of Hades will not prevail against it. I will give you the keys of the kingdom of heaven, and whatever you bind on earth will be bound in heaven, and whatever you loose on earth will be loosed in heaven."

Then he sternly ordered the disciples not to tell anyone that he was the Messiah. (Matthew 16:13–20, NRSV)

The kingdom of God comes in the world through Christ's *ekklesia*. "Ekklesia" is the Greek word translated "church" in our Bibles. Unfortunately, the word "church" doesn't accurately translate *"ekklesia."* "Church" most likely comes from *"kuriokos,"* which means "the house of the Lord." *Ekklesia* is much more than that.

The word *"ekklesia"* was first used in ancient Athens to describe the civic gathering of citizens to do the government business of the city-state. *Ekklesia* came into biblical usage around 250 BC when, according to some ancient Jewish sources (some scholars disagree), Ptolemy II Philadelphus commissioned seventy-two rabbis to translate the Hebrew Scriptures into Greek.

The rabbis chose *ekklesia* and *sunagoge* to translate "congregation" and "assembly." The "congregation" was all of Israel, but the "assembly" was when Israel gathered for a meeting. The rabbis used *ekklesia* and *sunagoge* interchangeably for the congregation, but when they rendered "assembly," they always used *ekklesia*.

The first use of *ekklesia* in the Hebrew Bible is when Israel is gathered at Sinai. The congregation (*sunagoge*) assembled (*ekklesia*) at Sinai to receive the law. From then on, when the congregation of Israel gathered in a meeting, it was considered an *ekklesia*.

By the time Jesus first used *ekklesia* in Matthew 16, the word had a long history within Israel. They, as did the Greeks before them, understood *ekklesia* to be a religious, governmental gathering where the people came to do the business of worship to the one true God and to govern the nation.

It is important to understand the dual religious and governmental nature of the *ekklesia* so that we do not reduce the *ekklesia* down to either merely a religious or a governmental gathering. It is both. The ancient world had no concept of our modern idea of "separation of church and state." The ancient Athenians would have seen the business of the state as service to the gods of the city. Israel would have viewed it exactly the same—to do political, governmental kingdom business was worship.

Upon This Rock

When Jesus declared that he would build his ekklesia on the rock, it would have been clear to those who heard him in the first century that he was gathering the congregation of Israel around him as Messiah.

Due to the timing of Daniel's prophecy, there were many "messiah movements" in the first century, and they all sent out a call for Israel to gather around them as Israel's true king, the Son of David, the one who would fulfill the prophets and restore the kingdom to Israel. The idea of a "counter-temple" movement that would gather Israel as ekklesia was not a novel idea.

This is how Israel would have seen John's baptisms at the Jordan River—a priest offering cleansing for the nation at the river instead of the temple, which had become corrupt through Sadducean collusion with Rome. The Essenes believed their ritual washings did the same.

Jesus announced that he was assembling true Israel around him, those who had a "revelation" from the Father of who Jesus really was. Jesus declared that he would build his ekklesia "on this rock," which was a multilayered reference to:

1. Mt. Hermon, the mountain looming over them, and the setting where the fallen angels gathered to rebel against the Most High. (Genesis 6, as interpreted by Jewish tradition.)

2. The "rock" that Daniel saw in the vision of Messiah's kingdom striking the clay feet of world empires, shattering and replacing them.

3. The "rock of revelation" that Jesus is the Israel's Messiah.

4. The "rock" of Simon Peter and the apostles, on whom the ekklesia would be founded.

The Gates of Death

Jesus then proclaimed boldly that "the gates of Hades will not prevail" against his ekklesia. The gates of Hades are the gates of death. (Remember, death was the ultimate enemy Jesus came to abolish. [2 Timothy 1:10]) The gates of Hades were the Grotto of Pan, a cave entrance near Caesarea Philippi (the city in which Jesus made this bold proclamation) where the debauched worship of Pan sought to appease the god of the underworld and avoid the horrors of punishment in the afterlife.

In a larger sense, the gates of death are the strongholds of sin and death that Satan, who dominated humans through the power of death (Hebrews 2:14), had erected within human society. Remember the *stoicheia*? Within the gates of death, the powers exert their control over humans through the fear of death, which means that the ingress and egress of human activity was controlled by the gates of death.

Jesus shattered the gates of death by dying and rising to live again. The resurrection of Jesus freed believers from the strongholds of hell. By infusing the Spirit of resurrection within the hearts of believers, Jesus delivered us from the fear of death.

Then, empowered by the Spirit and emboldened by the gospel of the kingdom, we carry the victory of Christ into the nations and overthrow the gates of death that evil powers have erected within the spirit-systems of the world. This is how the kingdom comes.

Envision, if you can, Jesus standing in the shadow of Mt. Hermon, where the powers had colluded against the Most High in Genesis 6, and looking down toward the Grotto of Pan, known as the Gates of Hell. Picture Jesus, his voice rising, pointing one finger at the mountain and another at the cave declaring, "Upon this rock—upon the mountain where the powers gathered against God!—I will build my ekklesia, and the gates of Hades—the deepest, darkest powers in the world!—will not prevail against it."

Powerful.

The Keys Of the Kingdom

Jesus told his disciples:

> *"I will give you the keys of the kingdom of heaven, and whatever you bind on earth will be bound in heaven, and whatever you loose on earth will be loosed in heaven." (Matthew 16:19)*

The keys *of* the kingdom ("of" not "to") are "the keys of Death and Hades" (Revelation 2:18; see also Revelation 9:1; 20:1) that Jesus claimed when he descended into the grave and then ascended into heaven to receive all authority in heaven and on earth—and even "under the earth" (Philippians 2:10).

The keys of the kingdom open the strongholds of death that have been erected by the powers within the hearts, homes and communities of fear-driven humans. The keys of the kingdom are the authority to bind and loose, especially to bind and loose the powers. (Revelation 9:1; 20:1) With the keys of the kingdom we can bind evil powers and unleash heaven on earth by unlocking "the gates of heaven" (Genesis 28:17).

The keys of the kingdom are also the "keys of David" (Revelation 3:7), the keys that open the treasury and armory of heaven.

The keys of the kingdom are "keywords." The keys we use are the words we speak. By preaching the gospel of the gospel, by prophesying and declaring God's truth in the face of every lie, we shatter the gates of death and release life. Learning and training people how to utilize praise, prayer and prophecy as the keys of the kingdom is the central task of the ekklesia.

(Again, see *Keywords* by Steve Pixler for an extended discussion of how our words are keys that open and close the gates of heaven and hell.)

Binding and Loosing

Jesus gave his disciples authority to bind and loose when they gather as ekklesia. (Which, by the way, only requires two believers to function as a governmental body. [Matthew 18:18-20]) Binding and loosing is executive, legislative and judicial authority all rolled into one.

Binding and loosing is simply the authority to permit and forbid. When believers bind and loose, they perform executive action, enact legislation and decide judicial matters. Binding and loosing are the governmental functions of the ekklesia.

However, it is important to correctly render the language Jesus used here. When he gave the ekklesia authority to bind and loose, the Greek phrasing he used is actually "whatever you bind on earth [having been] bound in heaven, and whatever you loose on earth [having been] loosed in heaven." The voice of the Greek verb phrases here indicates mutual action, decision in the present based on what has already been decided. The binding and loosing are done in collaboration. We bind and loose on earth in harmony with the will of heaven. Because we are seated in the heavens with Christ, the decisions made on earth are deliberated in concert with the Holy Spirit.

This is important to understand lest some believers think that they can snag a friend and force bad decisions on heaven. "God has to do whatever whatever Billy Bob and I bind on earth!" That's not how that works. We bind and loose in deliberation with the Divine Council. That's why the power to bind and loose is given to the ekklesia. The gathered faith community provides accountability and correction to prophetic action when needed. (1 Corinthians 14:29-33)

Restoring Ekklesia

As we noted above, the word "church" is a bad translation of *"ekklesia."* The ekklesia is the kingdom gathering of the disciples of Jesus. It is the governmental gathering of King Jesus and the citizens of heaven. The ekklesia is the parliament of King Jesus. The members of the ekklesia, like the Members of Parliament, each represent their own "area of influence" (2 Corinthians 9), their "metron," their parliamentary district.

The church, as we know it, has become a profoundly and tragically different thing than ekklesia. And we must restore ekklesia. Why? Because "church" is not working. The gates of hell are seemingly prevailing everywhere. Something is wrong. And what's wrong is that Jesus didn't come to build a "church"—he came to build his ekklesia. And there's a huge difference.

Why does it matter to you? Because ekklesia is where you get your keys! It is where you come into your "room," your "place," your "field."

What are we trying to accomplish? To better train believers to release the kingdom in to the world so that salvation comes to the nations.

What is the difference between a *church* and an *ekklesia*?

- A *church* is a religious institution where people worship, pray, hear the Word, give and fellowship.

- An *ekklesia* is a governmental, legislative assembly where believers gather to do the business of the kingdom, which includes worship, prayer, hearing the Word, giving and fellowship, but with a kingdom focus.

- Church is about having an *experience*. Ekklesia is about being *equipped*.
- Church is about "going to heaven." Ekklesia is about "your kingdom come."
- Church is about "clergy and laity" distinctions. Ekklesia is about equipping everyone.

The primary difference is that church is religious and ekklesia is legislative. The goal of church is to get people to heaven. The goal of ekklesia is to see the kingdom come in the world. The ekklesia is seated with the Divine Council of King Jesus through which the kingdom of God is released into the world.

In the traditional church, people gather as spectators, to watch a cast of religious professionals perform religious theater for their enjoyment. The ekklesia gathers for *all believers* to serve in priestly, prophetic and kingly roles so that they may carry that ministry out into their metron. In the ekklesia, all believers are transformed through the glory of God and then carry that glory into the world to release transformation in all nations.

The kingdom of God comes through personal transformation and the release of governmental authority from the ekklesia. As the kingdom comes in people, in families, and in the ekklesia, those equipped and empowered by the five-faceted ministry within the ekklesia take the kingdom out into their assigned area of influence.

When the ekklesia gathers, believers are trained to receive and exercise their authority. The five-faceted ministry distributes the keys of the kingdom. The apostles release the *apostolic;* the prophets release the *prophetic*; the evangelists release the *evangelistic*; the shepherds releases *shepherding*; and the teachers release *teaching.*

When believers go out into their assigned area of influence—their "metron," again, as Paul describes it in 2 Corinthians 10—they carry the giftings of the apostolic, prophetic, evangelistic, shepherding and teaching into their field.

(Read *Your Harvest Is In Your Field* by Steve Pixler for more on that.)

Every metron needs these five-faceted giftings.

• The apostolic releases the visionary, strategic, architecting gifts.

• The prophetic releases the future vision and insight, the spiritual intelligence, the ability to hear and declare intelligibly what God is saying.

• The evangelistic releases the *euangelion* gift that empowers every believer to share their faith and their story in a way that draws people to Christ.

• The shepherding releases love, compassion and empathy for people and their real life problems.

The shepherding gift prevents the gospel of the kingdom from becoming just an abstract theory that fails to take real people and real problems into account.

• The teaching releases the grace to teach and train others in the principles of the kingdom.

What happens in the ekklesia impacts the world. As we like to say, Sunday is about Monday. The way we encounter the glory of God determines what we carry into the world around us. As we've discussed above, cultural transformation starts with personal, familial and ecclesial transformation.

Why does it matter? Because the Father has given Christ all nations as his inheritance. Christ will receive his inheritance through his administration (*oikonomia*) in the ekklesia. Salvation and shalom will come to the nations through the ministry of the ekklesia.

Middleman Religion

What was the original ekklesia like?

1. The ekklesia gathered first around the table. (Luke 22; Acts 2:42, 46; 1 Co. 11-14)

2. They did have large gatherings, but the regular gatherings were in the home around the table, "reclining at table" in circles.

3. Everyone participated (1 Co. 14). There was no "clergy > laity" distinction. The five-faceted ministry equipped believers. (Ephesians 4)

What happened to the ekklesia? It changed from the table/council model to the basilica model along the lines of pagan temples and the Old Covenant temple. It created a clergy-laity distinction. It brought back "middleman religion."

In religion, humans tend to revert to the middleman. Through fear, humans ask "professionals" to do holy things for them so they don't get it wrong and die. Then the leaders ordained by God to equip the saints for works of service start doing the work for them.

This goes all the way back to Sinai:

When you heard the voice out of the darkness, while the mountain was burning with fire, you approached me, all the heads of your tribes and your elders; and you said, "Look, the Lord our God has shown us his glory and greatness, and we have heard his voice out of the fire. Today we have seen that God may speak to someone and the person may still live."

"So now why should we die? For this great fire will consume us; if we hear the voice of the Lord our God any longer, we shall die. For who is there of all flesh that has heard the voice of the living God

speaking out of fire, as we have, and remained alive?"

"Go near, you yourself, and hear all that the Lord our God will say. Then tell us everything that the Lord our God tells you, and we will listen and do it." (Deuteronomy 5:23–27, NRSV)

Paul referred to this in his letter to the churches of Galatia:

Why then the law? It was added because of transgressions, until the offspring would come to whom the promise had been made; and it was ordained through angels by a mediator. Now a mediator involves more than one party; but God is one. (Galatians 3:19–29, NRSV)

The writer of Hebrews also noted the problem with "middleman religion":

*You have not come to something that can be touched, a blazing fire, and darkness, and gloom, and a tempest, and the sound of a trumpet, and **a voice whose words made the hearers beg that not another word be spoken to them**. (For they could not endure the order that was given, "If even an animal touches the mountain, it shall be stoned to death." Indeed, so terrifying was the sight that Moses said, "I tremble with fear.")*

22 But you have come to Mount Zion and to the city of the living God, the heavenly Jerusalem, and to innumerable angels in festal gathering, 23 and to the assembly (ekklesia) of the firstborn who are enrolled in heaven, and to God the judge of all, and to the spirits of the righteous made perfect, 24 and to Jesus, the mediator of a new covenant, and to the sprinkled blood that speaks a better word than the blood of Abel. (Hebrews 12:18–24, NRSV)

A Kingdom That Cannot Be Shaken

The next section of Hebrews 12 gives us a direct contrast between middleman religion and the powerful heavenly-earthly ekklesia of King Jesus.

See that you do not refuse the one who is speaking; for if they did not escape when they refused the one who warned them on earth, how much less will we escape if we reject the one who warns from heaven! At that time his voice shook the earth; but now he has promised, "Yet once more I will shake not only the earth but also the heaven." This phrase, "Yet once more," indicates the removal of what is shaken—that is, created things—so that what cannot be shaken may remain.

Therefore, since we are receiving (paralambano) a kingdom that cannot be shaken, let us give thanks, by which we offer to God an acceptable worship with reverence and awe; for indeed our God is a consuming fire. (Hebrews 12:25–29, NRSV)

There is a powerful shaking going on in the world. God is shaking heaven and earth so that the institutional forms of religion may be removed and we may receive the kingdom that cannot be shaken. The old forms of "church" are being rocked by a seismic revelation: *the kingdom cannot come through dead religion.*

The kingdom is *"paralambano,"* which means to "receive by succession." The kingdom can only be received from the King. The kingdom cannot come through manmade religious institutions, which is what the church has become.

How do we "receive by succession" the kingdom?

(1) Hear the gospel (*euangelion*) of the kingdom (king's domain / heaven & earth, dominion restored).

(2) Baptized (inducted) into the ekklesia and seated in the King's government council.

(3) Equipped (authorized & empowered) by apostles, prophets, evangelists, shepherds and teachers to release the kingdom into our assigned areas of influence.

Why does ekklesia matter? Because the prayer, "Your kingdom come, your will be done in earth as it is in heaven," cannot happen apart from the ekklesia. The heavenly ekklesia is manifest in the earthly ekklesia when two or more gather and Christ becomes "the middle." The ekklesia is the portal through which the government of King Jesus is mediated into the earth.

The gospel of the kingdom is the only hope of the world. Jesus "through death destroyed him who had the power of death, that is the devil, and liberated those who were all their lifetime subject to slavery through the fear of death." That is the only hope for real change in the world. Salvation can only come to the nations through the death, burial, resurrection and ascension of King Jesus. The fact that Jesus is Lord is the hope of the world.

The ekklesia is the convened Divine Council of the ascended Christ through which he administers his *"oikonomia"* (his kingly administration) throughout the earth. The multiplication of ekklesia in the earth is Jesus' divine strategy for bringing his salvation to the nations. The *"euangelion"* (the gospel message) is the heart of evangelism. That is why it matters.

Ephesians: The Epic Ekklesia Epistle

We do not have enough time and space in a single unit to fully explore the ekklesia. Hopefully, this has been an adequate introduction, one that will pique your curiosity and provoke you to go on a quest for true ekklesia.

If you are interested in learning more about ekklesia, check out our other Continuum Ministry Resources on the ekklesia, books and courses that dig deeper. (stevepixler.com) But, most importantly, dive deep into *The Book of Ephesians,* Paul's epic masterpiece on the ekklesia.

In Ephesians you will learn how the ekklesia is seated together with Christ in the heavens; how the ekklesia is new cosmic temple of God, the dwelling place of God through the Spirit"; the gathering of both Jews and the nations in one body, the "one new man" of Ephesians 2; the display of manifold wisdom to the powers in Ephesians 3; the full grown man of Ephesians 4; and, in Ephesians 4-6, the means by which the world is being transformed through fierce spiritual warfare.

UNIT 9: TRANSFORMING CULTURE THROUGH MANIFEST GLORY

But the earth will be filled with the knowledge of the glory of the Lord, as the waters cover the sea. (Habakkuk 2:14, NRSV)

The kingdom of God is released into the world through the ekklesia. This is why what we do in the ekklesia and how we do it is such a big deal. The kingdom comes spiritually, gradually and fully when the ekklesia is functioning as intended.

The ultimate goal of the kingdom is that "the earth will be filled with the knowledge of the glory of the Lord, as the waters cover the sea" (Habakkuk 2:14, NRSV). The only way the glory of God can fill the earth is for the glory to first fill the ekklesia.

As Paul said, "the hope of glory" is "Christ in you" (Colossians 1:27). The "you" is plural, which means that the hope of glory in the earth is Christ within the community of believers. As the glory is released within the gathered ekklesia, individual believers carry the glory out into the world.

The Knowledge of the Glory

We often pray—and rightly so!—"your kingdom come, your will be done in earth as it is in heaven."

But the only way we can see the kingdom come "on earth as it is in heaven" is for us to experience heaven on earth when we gather as the ekklesia.

What is it like in heaven? It is an atmosphere of grace and glory. The grace of God is the goodness of God freely given, no strings attached. The glory of God is the *manifest attributes* of God. When we *glorify* the Lord, what we say about him begins to manifest.

We will look further at the grace of God in a moment. But for now, let's focus on glory.

Learning about glory, becoming "glory experts," is profoundly important. Only through "the *knowledge* of the glory of the Lord" can the earth be filled with his glory. We must study the glory.

One of the best examples of a glory environment is Isaiah 6. There are several things to note here:

(1) Isaiah saw the Lord in the year that King Uzziah died. (The end of an old era of politics and religion. We are currently witnessing another death of the old order.)

(2) The seraphim were above the throne. (The Mercy Seat is the throne of God and the angels form a "middle" in which God is enthroned.

(3) The angels cried, "Holy, holy, holy!" back and forth to one another. (They created a channel for the glory.)

We create an atmosphere of glory where his glory is released. We too often ask for glory to *fall* or to *come,* but in reality we have a synergistic role to play in creating a "middle" where glory is released. Worship releases glory.

Do you want to experience glory? Give him glory! When we gather to worship, we create a vortex (think shekinah cyclone) of glory between the worship team and the congregation, between you and the person standing beside you.

When we give God glory and honor, there is a release of power. (Glory + Honor = Power) Through our praise exchange and our testimony volley about his goodness, we create a channel for his mighty power to be known. From his throne of righteous judgment the Lord of Armies sends forth his angels to make war on our behalf.

The primary reason the ekklesia gathers is to combine and multiply our capacity for creating a "middle" (portal, gateway, Bethel) for the glory to flow from heaven to earth. It takes two to tango! Two or three gathered in Jesus' name (some say, two gather and Jesus is the third in the middle).

Why do we gather to worship? Because there is an *increase* (exponential) and *release* (channeling) of glory that happens when we gather two or more in his name. Our gathering becomes a glory gathering. Everyone in the room becomes a glory generator. When we cry, "Holy, holy, holy!" to each other, we create a *middle* for glory to be increased and released.

Then, as we are transformed by the glory, we become *transformers* that regulate and channel the release of glory. Glory generation becomes glory transmission.

(1) When we gather to give him glory, we are "**transformed** into his image from glory to glory" (2 Corinthians 3).

(2) Then, the glory of God flows out as **dominion** (crowned with glory and honor...work & worship) and manifests in the artifacts of culture (Psalm 8).

(3) When the world beholds the glory of God manifest in the children of God, creation is **liberated** from the curse (Romans 8). *Changed people change the world!* "Let it be on earth as it is in heaven."

(Want to know more? Read *Revelation Revolution* by Steve Pixler for more on how the glory liberates creation.)

Demystifying the Glory

One of the things we must do is "demystify the glory." The glory of God is simply the manifest attributes of God that become accessible to us when we glorify him. What we declare about God becomes *real*-ized when we worship him.

All the attributes of God can be categorized as *love* ("God is love"), *wisdom* ("Christ is the wisdom of God") and *power* ("you shall receive power after the Holy Spirit comes upon you").

The glory of God is simply the Father, Son and Spirit manifest as love, wisdom and power. The glory of God *is* God! (This is why we must never abstract or extract the attributes of God away from his personal presence and reduce glory down to a detached personal experience—like the "sign seekers.")

1. **Love**: the goodness of God, his kindness and affection. The love of God releases beauty, acceptance, affirmation, divine delight, pleasure, forgiveness, humility, on and on.

2. **Wisdom**: the knowledge of the Lord, insight, awareness, discernment, strategies, plans, future-sight (the prophetic), hindsight, intellect, intelligence, on and on.

3. **Power**: strength, might, ability, creativity, miracles, signs, wonders, divine intervention, capacity, endurance, on and on.

We are transformed in the glory as we experience love, wisdom and power, which corresponds directly to our triune being as the image of the triune God: emotions (love), mind (wisdom) and will (power). That's how we change.

And—once again!—changed people change the world. As we are transformed, we carry the glory of God into the real world, we release what we have received in the glory. We release:

1. **Love**: we release the love of God into a fear-filled world.
2. **Wisdom**: we bring solutions to real-world problems.
3. **Power**: we release supernatural power into impossible situations.

We become glory-carriers, and we take love, wisdom and power into our homes, workplaces and neighborhoods. Worship flows into work, and work becomes worship. That is how we fill the earth with his glory!

Grace and Truth

One of the most powerful things we have learned as we have pursued the glory of God is that *the glory of the Lord is only manifest in an environment of grace and truth*. To put it another way, legalism stifles the glory. Look at how John put it:

> *And the Word became flesh and lived among us, and we have seen his **glory**, the glory as of a father's only son, **full of grace and truth**.*
>
> *(John testified to him and cried out, "This was he of whom I said, 'He who comes after me ranks ahead of me because he was before me.'")*

*From his **fullness** we have all received, **grace upon grace**. The law indeed was given through Moses; **grace and truth** came through Jesus Christ.*

No one has ever seen God. It is God the only Son, who is close to the Father's heart, who has made him known. (John 1:14–18, NRSV)

The glory of God that transforms the nations flourishes in an environment of grace and truth.

- **Grace** is the kindness, favor and goodness of God freely given. "Grace" is also shorthand for "the gospel of grace," the message that our salvation is freely given in Christ apart from any effort we make.

*For by **grace** you have been saved through **faith**, and this is not your own doing; it is the gift of God —not the result of works, so that no one may boast. (Ephesians 2:8–9, NRSV)*

- **Truth** is believing the truth about God in contrast to believing the lies we have believed about him through law, religion and idolatry. ("Truth" here is *not* self-referential doctrinal truth.) Faith is believing the love of the Father—then, the truth about self and others.)

The law indeed was given through Moses; grace and truth came through Jesus Christ. No one has ever seen God. It is God the only Son, who is close to the Father's heart, who has made him known. (John 1:17-18, NRSV)

No one has ever seen God; if we love one another, God lives in us, and his love is perfected in us. By this we know that we abide in him and he in us, because he has given us of his Spirit.

And we have seen and do testify that the Father has sent his Son as the Savior of the world. God abides in those who confess that Jesus is the Son of God, and they abide in God. So we have known and believe the love that God has for us. (1 John 4:12–16, NRSV)

Knowing and believing the love of God is the *truth* that John is preaching. The increase and release of the glory of God cannot be sustained apart from this environment of grace and truth. Whenever revival happens—and "revival" is shorthand for the manifest glory of God—it almost always falters and fails because of religion and legalism. The environment of grace and truth is corrupted by law.

Note this: John directly contrasts "grace and truth" with "law." Law is the attempt to attain righteousness through what we do. ("Repentance from dead works…" [Hebrews 6:1]) In New Testament times it was circumcision, sabbath, food laws and other regulations given to Israel to separate and preserve the lineage of Messiah and transmit "the oracles of God." In our day, it is the rules of religion. Paul calls it "flesh." And no flesh may glory in his presence.

Do we want to increase and release the glory? Then we must militantly preserve an environment of grace and truth.

The Fullness of the Earth Is His Glory

It is not enough just to behold the glory of the Lord: we must be changed by it. But it is also not enough just to be changed: we must release that change into the world. Once more, changed people change the world.

This idea is embodied in Isaiah 6. Look at the last phrase: "The whole earth is full of his glory." There are three ways to render this phrase from the Hebrew into English:

1. "The whole earth is full of his glory."

2. "Let (cause) the earth be full of his glory."

3. "The fullness of the earth is his glory."

The idea of filling the earth with his glory goes all the way back to Genesis 1:

God blessed them, and God said to them, "Be fruitful and multiply, and fill the earth and subdue it; and have dominion over the fish of the sea and over the birds of the air and over every living thing that moves upon the earth." (Genesis 1:28, NRSV)

God created the world and set humans in dominion over the earth to steward it in partnership with him. God intended for humans to bring forth the fullness of the earth working with God. God pours out the rain, makes the sun to shine and gives life to the seed. Humans break open the soil, plant the seed and employ wise cultivation techniques to bring forth more fruitfulness. Through this process of divine-human cooperation, the earth brings forth its latent fullness. This is called dominion.

And God is glorified in dominion. God created humans and "crowned them with glory and honor and gave them dominion over the works of [his] hands" (Psalm 8:5-6). God created humans to bear his image and share his glory through divine-human partnership over the earth.

Humans were created to develop the latent potential within the earth and develop it into glorious works that would display the glory of God from Eden to the New Jerusalem. Humans were created to cultivate the earth's agricultural, biological, zoological, anthropological, economic, literary, medical, political, scientific, technological fullness, on and on.

Glory is supremely practical. Too often we marginalize (we actually *heaven-ize*) glory and fail to see how it manifests in the artifacts of culture. The glory of God is manifest in music, art, literature, architecture, culinary arts, fashion, horticulture, medicine, education, politics (when godly rulers lead!), judiciary (when justice reigns!), space exploration, technology—anywhere that beauty and function merge to manifest divine-human creativity.

The angels do not sing that *heaven* shall be full of his glory—it already is! They sing that the *earth* shall be filled with his glory. And we are the *only ones* who can release that glory into the earth. "Making the world a better place" begins with worship. Society's "mountain influencers" are transformed by his glory. We must reclaim the unreligious, "worldly" purpose of worship, the everyday, practical purpose of glory. Worship is meant to fill ordinary, mundane life with the glory of God. The glory of the Lord must fill every sphere of human society in order to "make the world a better place."

How does that happen? The glory of the Lord is increased and released when we gather to worship. We are transformed in the glory of God, and we carry the glory out into our metrons. As the influencers of society, we are deputized as glory-carriers when we gather to worship.

The Gold and the Glory

Haggai 2 demonstrates how practical and "this-worldly" the glory of God really is. It shows us that the glory of God is not just an ethereal, abstract "feeling" or "manifestation" in the presence of God. The glory of God is meant to take form and manifest within the physical world. The glory manifests in the artifacts of culture.

Take a look.

For thus says the Lord of hosts: Once again, in a little while, I will shake the heavens and the earth and the sea and the dry land; and I will shake all the nations, so that the treasure of all nations shall come, and I will fill this house with splendor (kabod, glory), says the Lord of hosts.

The silver is mine, and the gold is mine, says the Lord of hosts. The latter splendor (kabod, glory) of this house shall be greater than the former, says the Lord of hosts; and in this place I will give prosperity (shalom), says the Lord of hosts. (Haggai 2:6–9, NRSV)

Haggai 2 shows a direct connection between gold—yes, actually, the physical gold!—and the glory of God. When God declares that he will fill the "latter house" with glory, he explains that the glory he's speaking about includes silver and gold, "the treasure of all nations."

When God declares that he will fill the latter house (the living temple, the ekklesia, the cosmos) with glory by bringing into it all the treasures of the nations, he highlights a powerful fact: when the earth is filled with the glory of God, it will include world economies. The fullness of the earth includes world economies, both its tangible and intangible wealth.

As we shall see, one of the biggest shakeups happening in the world right now is a divine "shakedown." There is a global, cosmic battle going on right now between King Jesus, his holy angels, the awakened Christians and the global power of Mammon. If we truly hope to see the kingdom come in the real world, then the kingdom must come in world economies.

Without the slightest hint of embarrassment, Haggai 2 makes an explicit connection between the gold of the earth and the glory of God. As God fills his house with glory, he will bring the treasures of all nations into his house. World economies will bow to Christ as the kingdoms of this world become the kingdoms of God and his Christ. It's all about economic alignment. Heaven on earth.

The "gold and the glory" idea is rooted in Genesis 2 where Scripture highlights the fact that there was gold in the land:

> *A river flows out of Eden to water the garden, and from there it divides and becomes four branches. The name of the first is Pishon; it is the one that flows around the whole land of Havilah, where there is gold; and the gold of that land is good; bdellium and onyx stone are there. (Genesis 2:10–12, NRSV)*

Eden had gold in the ground. In Eden, the gold was raw materials. By the time we arrive at the end of the Bible, Revelation 21-22, the gold in the ground has been mined, purified and developed into the City of Gold, the New Jerusalem. (The parallels between the Garden and the Garden City are explicit and deliberate.) Eden is the world in its pristine, undeveloped state. The New Jerusalem portrays what the world looks like when the latent potential of the earth has been finally and fully developed.

Along the way, the Creator's gold was used to craft idols. The golden calf and Babylon became rivals systems, false world economies that challenge Christ's lordship over the earth. But the gold God hid in the ground was meant originally and finally to reveal the glory of the Lord.

And it shall do so. As God said in Haggai 2, "The silver is mine, and the gold is mine, says the Lord of hosts." The zeal of the Lord of Armies will perform it.

Kingdom Economics

The kingdom comes through sanctified finances. God redeems the economies of the world through kingdom stewardship. There are two economies within the world: Caesar vs. Christ, which is also God vs. Mammon. When we submit our wealth to Christ and bring it into partnership with God through the Holy Spirit, we redeem "unrighteous mammon" and transfer it to Christ's kingdom economy.

God redeems the wealth of the wicked through Spirit-led *giving, earning, saving* and *investing*. Every dollar that passes through the hands of covenant givers is sanctified. As more and more of the world's wealth is transferred to the righteous, the spirit of Mammon is broken.

Just as the glory of God in the ekklesia flourishes only in an environment of grace and truth, so kingdom finance flourishes only in an environment of grace and truth. Therefore, God is recruiting kingdom financiers who are led by grace, not law, in their giving. No legalistic giving allowed. Our giving must be Spirit-led.

We do not give because God needs the money. We give because we need God in our money. We need the infusion of grace in our finances. We need financial redemption. When we give into kingdom causes, we bring our finances under the Lordship of Jesus and into dominion partnership with God.

Paul understood the power of strategic breakthrough giving. When he mobilized the Gentile churches to send relief to the Jewish church in Jerusalem, he was profoundly conscious of how their giving could shift the narrative and the balance of power within the church and thus the world.

> *The point is this: the one who sows sparingly will also reap sparingly, and the one who sows bountifully will also reap bountifully. Each of you must give as you have made up your mind, not reluctantly or under compulsion, for God loves a cheerful giver.*

And God is able to provide you with every blessing in abundance, so that by always having enough of everything, you may share abundantly in every good work. As it is written, "He scatters abroad, he gives to the poor; his righteousness endures forever."

He who supplies seed to the sower and bread for food will supply and multiply your seed for sowing and increase the harvest of your righteousness. You will be enriched in every way for your great generosity, which will produce thanksgiving to God through us; for the rendering of this ministry not only supplies the needs of the saints but also overflows with many thanksgivings to God.

Through the testing of this ministry you glorify God by your obedience to the confession of the gospel of Christ and by the generosity of your sharing with them and with all others, while they long for you and pray for you because of the surpassing grace of God that he has given you.

Thanks be to God for his indescribable gift! (2 Corinthians 9:6–15)

This is the sort of strategic kingdom breakthrough giving that Holy Spirit is releasing in and through us. No doubt we need money to operate our ekklesia. And there is great power released through honor, which always has a financial component. But we are after more than just increasing contributions. We are after breakthrough giving, giving that breaks the strongholds of poverty and the spirit of mammon.

The Windows of Heaven

Malachi 3 is a key, kingdom economy passage. Though we must repudiate the legalistic tithe (we will talk about grace-based tithing another time), for now you must see a powerful principle regarding kingdom economics.

God promised his people that, as they entered into financial partnership with him through the tithe, he would "open the windows of heaven and pour out a blessing you cannot contain." The windows of heaven are often understood to mean the opening of the skies to pour out rain. And that is certainly valid. But the windows are much more than just rainfall.

Windows are a metaphor for revelation. We must ascend Bethel's ladder and look into the heavens to see giving from God's vantage point. We must be delivered from an earthbound perspective on giving. But once we ascend, we are seated with Christ in the heavenly places, where we now look back out of heaven's windows to see the world below from God's perspective.

We look through windows to see the world beyond. As we are seated with Christ in heavenly places (the ekklesia), we are drawn into a heavenly perspective on world economies. We develop kingdom investment strategies to advance and finance the Great Commission—which is much more than just traditional "missions"—in collaboration with the Divine Council. We fully embrace Spirit-led giving.

When we view world economies through the windows of heaven, we see finance from heaven's point of view. How does our perspective change when we view finance and world economies through the windows of heaven?

- We see from *faith, not fear*.
- We see from *generosity, not greed*.
- We embrace *inclusion, not exclusion*.
- We see *opportunities, not oppression*.
- We see *outcomes, not incomes (outflow, not intake)*.

The cosmos cannot be saved without the economies of the world being saved. Whoever controls the purse strings controls the world. Political, religious and cultural corruption always follows money and power. The salvation of the world and the shalom of the nations is directly tied to economic justice. And economic justice cannot be achieved through political or economic force—it can *only* be achieved through the freedom of grace-based, Spirit-led finance.

Our loving, exile-repatriating Abba Father plans to bring the economies of the world under the dominion of King Jesus until the fullness of the earth becomes his manifest glory through kingdom prosperity (on earth as it is in heaven).

Father God is not just harnessing economies: he is harnessing all the spheres of human society. But world economies are specifically in view in this new kingdom era. This is particularly true here in Mansfield and within our ecclesial assignment. We are called to break "the old spirit of injustice" that has given room to the spirit of mammon, the spirit of poverty that embargoes wealth and reserves the shalom prosperity of the city for the elite.

From its founding as a community and city, God has enlisted the fruitful fields of Mansfield to be a world center for kingdom financiers, for givers who are more than mere donors. God is looking for partners!

(That is where grace-based, Spirit-led tithing comes in. Be watching for a new book coming soon called *The Windows of Heaven* where we will explore non-legalistic, grace-based, Spirit-led kingdom tithing.)

God is recruiting kingdom financiers to Mansfield. And these financiers will fund kingdom advance around the world. The Spirit says that God has destined Mansfield to fund the kingdom since before it was founded, but the spirit of mammon took root at its inception and bent the wealth of this city to the inurement of a few. That is over. The kingdom has come.

Now, Father God is delivering the economy of this city so that it may become a signal city, a prototype, a New Jerusalem, heaven on earth. Significant transformation will come to this city as a result. There will be much shaking. And God will shake this city in order to loose its wealth for his kingdom. God is making this city a center for economic transformation. He is drawing kingdom financiers to this city who will fund the kingdom (not just church) around the world.

Even more significantly, Mansfield has been selected by the Spirit as an epicenter for financial growth among minorities, among First Nations, Black, Hispanic and Asian families. The Spirit has been saying for a while now that King Jesus has decreed kingdom reparations for those who have been economically disadvantaged through economic injustice since Mansfield's founding in 1856. The reparations that King Jesus has ordered are not dependent on political realities and will not arise from vengeance. His reparations will flow from heaven as he harnesses the wealth of the wicked and redirects it to his once-oppressed children.

Watch and see what God will do.

Freedom Life Church and any other ekklesia that catches the vision and spirit of what God is doing will become centers of economic transformation where business, civic and community leaders will be trained to release his glory in the earth.

God is recruiting breakthrough givers to the City of Mansfield and to Freedom Life Church. He is summoning people who will be more than contributors or donors. He is calling people who will be seated with him in heavenly places viewing finance through heaven's windows and become partners with him in kingdom investment. Kingdom investors and kingdom financiers are people who invest strategically in people, churches, non-profits, businesses and philanthropy through Spirit-led giving.

The invitation to give at Freedom Life is not just a matter of meeting our operations budget. Giving here is breakthrough giving that is breaking the spirit of Mammon and shattering the "old spirit of injustice" that has embargoed the wealth of this city for the benefit of a few. That's over. In Jesus' name!

God Will Fulfill All Your Needs

Paul draws a direct line between God supplying all our needs and his riches in glory. Do you see the relation between riches and glory? Look at it:

> *And this same God who takes care of me will supply all your needs from his glorious riches, which have been given to us in Christ Jesus. (Philippians 4:19, NLT)*

And the NIV:

And my God will meet all your needs according to his glorious riches in Christ Jesus. (Philippians 4:19, NIV84)

God will supply all of our needs *from* his glorious riches in Christ.

The word "supply" is "*plerosei,*" which means "to fill up," or "fulfill." It is literally "bring to fullness"!

Our "need" is the arena where his "fullness" is displayed. Our need—our lack—is t*he matrix of fullness*. Right where the ground seems uncultivated and unfruitful, we sink our plow and bring forth fullness.

The fullness of the earth comes in the intersection of our need and his provision. This is literally the "breakthrough of glory into our need." Christ's glory, his glorious riches, are manifest in fullness as provision.

The glory of Christ breaks through from heaven into earth. But what really fascinates me is that the glory of Christ is manifest as wealth. And Paul also emphasizes the circle of glory here, the glory-exchange: the glory of Christ flows through heaven's provision and invades the point of our need. And as his provision breaks through into the earth to bring fullness where need had been, we then give glory to God.

Which brings us to the final praise in verse twenty: "To our God and Father be glory forever and ever. Amen."

God is not glorified by poverty. He is not glorified by intractable needs that are never met. He is not glorified when we suffer with lack. He is glorified when the need becomes the arena of provision. The barren land brings forth. And that brings glory to God—for "the fullness of the earth is his glory." (Isaiah 6)

King Jesus is calling for kingdom partners, for those who ascend into heavenly places in the ekklesia and view world economies through the windows of heaven. He is calling for visionary givers, for breakthrough givers who see their giving as breaking the spirit of mammon that has suffocated the wealth of the earth by reserving it for the few, for global elites. It is time for the fullness of the earth to become the glory of the One who created every individual on the planet to bring forth the fullness and the shalom of the earth.

The Spirit is calling on us to become kingdom partners. And here is the proviso: we must be more than just donors. We must be Spirit-led investors. If you tithe, you must repudiate legalistic tithing—tithing because you "have to." No, you must become a Spirit-led tither.

That means that, though we all accept our primary responsibility to fund the ekklesia where we are trained and to honor those who father and mother us spiritually, we may be directed by Holy Spirit to invest our giving in needs outside the local church. And we must become willing to give above the tenth. We must be bold enough to trust the leading of the Spirit. Only Spirit-led giving can bust the spirit of Mammon.

The kingdom of God cannot come fully in the earth without world economies coming under the Lordship of King Jesus. When Jesus describes the two "masters" of the world, he doesn't say, "God or the devil..." He says, "God or mammon." That's how significant the battle for economic dominion really is. (There are two competing economies: Christ/Caesar, God/Mammon) As the kingdom of God comes in the world, God promised to transfer the wealth of nations into his kingdom.

How does God transfer the wealth of the wicked into the kingdom? Through kingdom-principled stewardship (*Spirit-led giving, earning, spending, saving & investing.*) Grace-based giving is the kingdom instrument used to transfer wealth from mammon to God. Spirit-led giving redeems money.

Again, we do not give because God needs the money. We give because *we need God in our money*. We need the infusion of grace in our finances. We need economic redemption.

The powers of darkness wield control over the world through corrupt money. The redemption of world economies is absolutely central to "your kingdom come, your will be done in earth as it is in heaven." There is no real change in the world apart from the redemption of money. Without it, the world always reverts back corrupt, power-based systems. (Follow the money!)

Giving is spiritual warfare.

Cultural Transformation

As "Christ in you (all), the hope of glory" fills believers and believers fill the earth, the knowledge of the glory of the Lord shall fill the earth as the waters cover the sea. (Habakkuk 2:14, NRSV) Every sphere of human existence will be influenced through love, wisdom and power (supernatural power, not violent power), and the powers will be subdued in every nation. The ekklesia will grow into the "habitation of God by the Spirit," the "one new man" made up of restored Israel and the redeemed nations, into "the measure of the stature of the fullness of Christ."

This takes us into the next unit where we will look at the texts that shape our eschatological expectation. These passages will confirm what we have asserted so boldly: *changed people change the world!* These upcoming passages will show that the kingdom of God will come spiritually, gradually and fully prior to the return of Christ and the resurrection of the dead.

MODULE 4: ESCHATOLOGY & EXPECTATION

UNIT 10: KEY TEXTS THAT SHAPE OUR EXPECTATION

The kingdom has come. The kingdom is coming. Which is true? Both.

The tension between how much the kingdom has already come and how much its coming happens after the Second Coming is the heart of kingdom discussion. Bible scholars usually call this "the already/not yet" aspect of the kingdom.

There is no doubt that Jesus declared that the kingdom had already broken in upon the world when he performed signs and wonders. (Luke 11:20) And there are numerous passages that set forth a powerful expectation that the kingdom of God will see profound victory in the world prior to the end of history. The Great Commission is not wishful thinking. But it is also true that the New Testament is filled with future-hope promises about the consummation of the kingdom and the age to come.

Kingdom Inauguration and Consummation

How do we balance all this? Simply by understanding the *inauguration* and the *consummation* of the kingdom. The events surrounding what is often called "The First Advent" are inaugural kingdom events. From the birth of Jesus, to his life and ministry, to his death, burial and resurrection, to his ascension, to Pentecost, to Christ's "coming in judgment" upon Jerusalem in AD 70—all these are *inaugural,* First Advent events. The First Advent is a complex series of events that launched the kingdom in time and space.

The Second Advent is the *consummation* of the kingdom. The Second Advent is also a complex series of events including the final victory over the powers; the resurrection with its final, full victory over the last enemy, death; the liberation of creation; the descent of the New Jerusalem; the manifest unity of heaven and earth; the New Heavens and New Earth fully realized; the visible presence of King Jesus in the new creation; and—most of all!—the triune God, all in all, in everything.

The "First Advent/Second Advent," *inauguration/consummation,* "already/not yet" language can help us clarify how to think about the extent of kingdom victory in the world here and now. So hold on to those phrases.

Is Jesus Coming Soon?

One of the key questions that shapes how Christians see the kingdom within history is the question of Jesus' return. Is Jesus coming soon, or will there be a continued delay? That's a good question! Let's talk about it.

First, a quick vocabulary lesson. There are a couple of words that are often used to describe how people think about the end of history. One is *eschatology*. It simply means "the doctrine of last things," from the Greek word *"eschatos."*

The second word is *apocalypse* (with its first cousin, *apocalyptic*). It comes from the Greek word *"apokalupto,"* and it means "unveiling, revelation." It is used in the Greek title of *The Book of Revelation*, which is why Revelation is often called "The Apocalypse." Matthew 24 is often called "The Little Apocalypse."

The way people view events at the end of history is described as their *eschatology*. The entire genre of end of the world expectations is called *apocalyptic*.

Eschatological and apocalyptic expectations have fascinated Christians since the first century. But since the 1800s, eschatology and apocalyptic have seized Christian imagination and dogma like never before. The rise of an eschatological system called *dispensationalism*, from the 1830s to its peak in the mid-twentieth century, popularized and dogmatized the expectation of Christ's return in an unprecedented way, primarily in American Christianity.

The expectation of "the soon return of Christ" in a visible, bodily Second Coming became a key doctrine within fundamentalism. Though there were varying opinions on the timing of events surrounding Christ's return, the idea that "Jesus is coming soon!"

took root in evangelical doctrine. Fringe eschatology became fundamental theology.

But is Jesus coming soon? It is certainly possible. As I often say, "Jesus could come before I finish… [long pause]…this sentence. [Another pause, look around.] But he didn't." My point is not just to be cute. It is to highlight the reality that one persons's interpretation of Scripture does not bind God. He could come at any time, and everyone's eschatology would have to adjust to fit his will.

Obviously.

Yet there are good, biblical reasons to believe that Jesus is not coming soon. In this unit, let's take a moment to rush through a passel of scriptures that indicate a degree of victory for Christ's kingdom within history that hasn't happened yet.

Key Texts That Shape Our Expectation

It will be necessary due to time and space to skim these passages a bit. But, hopefully, we can get a decent overview. Let's start with two passages in Acts.

Acts 1:1-11

> *1 In the first book, Theophilus, I wrote about all that Jesus did and taught from the beginning 2 until the day when he was taken up to heaven, after giving instructions through the Holy Spirit to the apostles whom he had chosen.*

3 After his suffering he presented himself alive to them by many convincing proofs, appearing to them during forty days and **speaking about the kingdom of God***.*

4 While staying with them, he ordered them not to leave Jerusalem, but to wait there for the promise of the Father. "This," he said, "is what you have heard from me; 5 for John baptized with water, but you will be baptized with the Holy Spirit not many days from now."

6 **So when they had come together, they asked him, "Lord, is this the time when you will restore the kingdom to Israel?"** *7 He replied, "It is not for you to know the times or periods that the Father has set by his own authority. 8 But you will receive power when the Holy Spirit has come upon you; and* **you will be my witnesses in Jerusalem, in all Judea and Samaria, and to the ends of the earth***."*

9 When he had said this, as they were watching, he was lifted up, and a cloud took him out of their sight. 10 While he was going and they were gazing up toward heaven, suddenly two men in white robes stood by them. 11 They said, "Men of Galilee, why do you stand looking up toward heaven? This Jesus, who has been taken up from you into heaven, will come in the same way as you saw him go into heaven." Acts 1:1–11, NRSV)

There are three key points here:

1. Jesus spent forty days with his disciples after his resurrection explaining what he had taught them about the kingdom of God.

2. Jesus' teaching on the kingdom was driven by their question concerning the restoration of the kingdom to Israel.

3. Jesus' made it clear that the kingdom would come spiritually, gradually and fully.

Point 3 is the one we must absorb most deeply. Look at Acts 1:8:

But you will receive power when the Holy Spirit has come upon you; and you will be my witnesses in Jerusalem, in all Judea and Samaria, and to the ends of the earth."

This verse shows that the kingdom would come *spiritually*: "But you will receive power when the Holy Spirit has come upon you."

It shows that the kingdom would come *gradually*: "You will be my witnesses in Jerusalem, in all Judea and Samaria, and to the ends of the earth." Obviously, it would take time to expand Christian witness in this way.

And then this verse shows that the kingdom will come *fully*: "To the ends of the earth." As we mentioned above, this is a quote from Psalm 2: "Ask of me, and I will make the nations your heritage, and the ends of the earth your possession" (Psalm 2:8, NRSV).

What's the point? Jesus will not return until "the ends of the earth" are his possession.

Acts 3:19-21

The second passage in Acts is in Acts 3 where Peter preached to the crowd that gathered after the lame man was healed.

> *19 Repent therefore, and turn to God so that your sins may be wiped out, 20 **so that times of refreshing may come from the presence of the Lord**, and **that he may send the Messiah appointed for you**, that is, Jesus, 21 **who must remain in heaven until the time of universal restoration** that God announced long ago through his holy prophets." (Acts 3:19–21, NRSV)*

There are two things here that must precede Christ's return.

1. The "times of refreshing" (a euphemism for Israel's spiritual renewal foretold by the prophets) must "come from the presence of the Lord" before God will "send the Messiah appointed for you."

2. The "universal restoration" (*apokatastasis*) foretold by the prophets must happen first. Jesus "must remain in heaven" until that happens. As we have seen already and will continue to see, "the time of universal restoration" doesn't happen suddenly when Jesus returns. It happens gradually, over time. And when the time—the

"fullness of time"—has been fulfilled, then Jesus will return.

Romans 8:18–25

In Romans 8, Paul describes what happens at the climax of human history, when the resurrection of believers precipitates the liberation of all creation. This is one of the "already, but not yet" passages that points us toward a *consummation* reality that will not happen until Jesus returns.

> *18 I consider that the sufferings of this present time are not worth comparing with **the glory about to be revealed to [in] us**. 19 For the **creation waits with eager longing for the revealing of the children of God**; 20 for the creation was subjected to futility, not of its own will but by the will of the one who subjected it, in hope 21 that the **creation itself will be set free from its bondage to decay and will obtain the freedom of the glory of the children of God**.*
>
> *22 We know that the whole creation has been groaning in labor pains until now; 23 and not only the creation, but we ourselves, who have the first fruits of the Spirit, groan inwardly **while we wait for adoption, the redemption of our bodies**.*
>
> *24 For in hope we were saved. Now hope that is seen is not hope. For who hopes for what is seen? 25 But if we hope for what we do not see, we*

wait for it with patience. (Romans 8:18–25, NRSV)

The key statement here is "while we wait for adoption, the redemption of our bodies." This indicates that Paul is referring to the resurrection when our bodies are glorified, when "this mortal puts on immortality and this corruptible puts on incorruption" (1 Corinthians 15:53), when we are "clothed with our heavenly dwelling," our "ageless body." (2 Corinthians 5:1-5)

Though it is true that coming reality of a renewed cosmos can begin to be experienced here and now as an anticipation of the age to come, the fullness of cosmic liberation awaits the resurrection of believers.

(See Steve Pixler, *Revelation Revolution* for more on Romans 8.)

Romans 11:25–36

Paul's teaching on the faithfulness of God in and through the faithlessness of Israel gives us one of the best timelines of expectation in the New Testament.

Take a look.

25 So that you may not claim to be wiser than you are, brothers and sisters, **I want you to understand this mystery: a hardening has come upon part of Israel, until the full number of the Gentiles has come in.** *26 And so* **all Israel will be saved**; *as it is* *written, "Out of Zion will come the Deliverer; he will banish ungodliness from Jacob." 27 "And this is my covenant with them, when I take away their sins."*

28 As regards the gospel they are enemies of God for your sake; but as regards election they are beloved, for the sake of their ancestors; 29 **for the gifts and the calling of God are irrevocable**.

30 Just as you were once disobedient to God but have now received mercy because of their disobedience, 31 so they have now been disobedient in order that, by the mercy shown to you, they too may now receive mercy. 32 **For God has imprisoned all in disobedience so that he may be merciful to all**.

33 O the depth of the riches and wisdom and knowledge of God! How unsearchable are his judgments and how inscrutable his ways! 34 "For who has known the mind of the Lord? Or who has been his counselor?" 35 "Or who has given a gift to him, to receive a gift in return?" 36 For from him and through him and to him are all things. To him be the glory forever. Amen.

The timeline in Romans 11 is clear. (Go back and read Romans 9-11 when you can to get the full context.) A remnant of Israel believed on Christ, and the remainder were hardened. They were hardened, as Paul put it, so that "through their fall salvation could come to the Gentiles." But God, in his mercy, plans to use the salvation of the Gentiles to restore salvation to Israel. And here's the key:

"A hardening has come upon part of Israel, until the full number of the Gentiles has come in. And so all Israel will be saved."

The "full number" of the Gentiles is the Greek word *"pleroma."* It simply means "fullness." It was used to describe a full harvest (of olive trees, for example), a full cargo on a ship, etc.

Do you get what Paul is saying? When the *pleroma* of *ta ethne* (the Gentiles, the nations) has come to Christ—when the nations been have repatriated!—then the fullness of the Gentiles will be the catalyst for Israel's turning, for her return to Christ as Messiah.

Earlier in Romans 11, Paul referenced Moses' prophecy that Israel would be provoked to jealousy by "a people who are not a people"—the Gentiles. When the Gentiles come to *pleroma,* it will be obvious that the blessing of Abraham's covenant is upon them. The Jews, who will never cease to be God's covenant people ("the gifts and callings of God of irrevocable"), will experience "the times of refreshing that come from the Lord" and their hearts will be turned. The broken away Jewish branches will be re-grafted into the Abrahamic olive tree.

What does this mean with regard to Christ's return? Jesus will not return until the fullness of the

Gentiles becomes the catalyst for Israel's restoration. As this hasn't happened yet (though there is certainly a move of God among Israel with many Jews turning to Christ), Christ's return is not yet imminent.

1 Corinthians 15:20–28

Paul gives another clear eschatological timeline in 1 Corinthians 15.

> *20 But in fact Christ has been raised from the dead, the first fruits of those who have died. 21 For since death came through a human being, the resurrection of the dead has also come through a human being; 22 for as all die in Adam, so all will be made alive in Christ. 23 But each in his own order: Christ the first fruits, then at his coming those who belong to Christ.*
>
> *24 Then comes the end, when he hands over the kingdom to God the Father, after he has destroyed every ruler and every authority and power. 25 For he must reign until he has put all his enemies under his feet. 26 The last enemy to be destroyed is death. 27 For "God has put all things in subjection under his feet." But when it says, "All things are put in subjection," it is plain that this does not include the one who put all things in subjection under him.*
>
> *28 When all things are subjected to him, then the Son himself will also be subjected to the one who*

put all things in subjection under him, so that God may be all in all. (1 Corinthians 15:20–28, NRSV)

There's a million things to explore in this passage, but just one that we must highlight: Jesus must reign from the heavens at the right hand of the Father until God has "destroyed every ruler and every authority and power," until the Father has "put all his enemies under his feet."

The key word here is "until." Jesus must reign from the heavens "until" all the powers are subdued. Many popular eschatologies argue that Jesus will subdue his enemies all at once when he returns. But that is *not* what Paul said. He specifically argued that Jesus would remain seated at the right hand of the Father "until" all his enemies were placed under his feet.

Hebrews 10 says the same thing:

But when Christ had offered for all time a single sacrifice for sins, "he sat down at the right hand of God," and since then has been waiting "until his enemies would be made a footstool for his feet." For by a single offering he has perfected for all time those who are sanctified. (Hebrews 10:12–14, NRSV)

Paul is clear. The powers will be subdued while Jesus is seated at the Father's right hand. This is based on Psalm 110: "The Lord says to my lord, 'Sit at my right hand until I make your enemies your footstool.'" And, after God the Father has subdued Christ's enemies by the omnipresenced authority of Christ mediated through his body, the ekklesia, then "the last enemy to be destroyed is death."

Here's another clear point in the timeline. When will death be finally and fully destroyed? At the resurrection of believers.

> *When this perishable body puts on imperishability, and this mortal body puts on immortality, then the saying that is written will be fulfilled: "Death has been swallowed up in victory." "Where, O death, is your victory? Where, O death, is your sting?" The sting of death is sin, and the power of sin is the law. But thanks be to God, who gives us the victory through our Lord Jesus Christ. (1 Corinthians 15:54–57, NRSV)*

So many Christians have been trained to believe that Jesus will return and defeat evil once for all all at once. But that is not what Paul believed. The subduing of Christ's enemies happens gradually. It is so easy to imitate the Pharisees of Jesus day who thought the kingdom would "immediately appear" and develop an eschatology that puts the onus on Jesus and rests smugly in the idea that the devil will get what's coming to him when our big brother gets back in town.

But the goal of Jesus' and Paul's teaching on the kingdom was to show us our synergistic, collaborative responsibility to work with Christ in the subduing of his enemies. Jesus is not coming to do our homework for us. The authority and responsibility to advance the kingdom and subdue the powers is on us—actually, *in us:* Christ in us, the hope of glory.

Ephesians 2:15-16; 21-22; 3:1-13

As mentioned earlier, Ephesians is the epic ecclesial epistle. (We need to develop a full course on just Ephesians. Be watching for that.)

In Ephesians 2, Paul gives another eschatological expectation: *When Jews and Gentiles are gathered fully into "one new man," then the body of Christ will become the completed cosmic temple, the "habitation of God through the Spirit"* (Ephesians 2:22, KJV)

Here's the context:

He has abolished the law with its commandments and ordinances, that he might create in himself one new humanity in place of the two, thus making peace, and might reconcile both groups to God in one body through the cross, thus putting to death that hostility through it. (Ephesians 2:15–16, NRSV)

In him the whole structure is joined together and grows into a holy temple in the Lord; in whom you also are built together spiritually into a dwelling place for God. (Ephesians 2:21-22, NRSV)

Jesus will not return until the temple is finished. And the temple will not be finished until the Jews and Gentiles are gathered together in one new humanity.

Paul calls this union of Jews and Gentiles "the mystery of Christ." Look at how Paul put it in Ephesians 3:

> *This is the reason that I Paul am a prisoner for Christ Jesus for the sake of you Gentiles—2 for surely you have already heard of the commission of God's grace that was given me for you, 3 and how **the mystery** was made known to me by revelation, as I wrote above in a few words, 4 a reading of which will enable you to perceive my understanding of **the mystery of Christ**.*
>
> *5 In former generations this **mystery** was not made known to humankind, as it has now been revealed to his holy apostles and prophets by the Spirit: 6 that is, **the Gentiles have become fellow heirs, members of the same body, and sharers in the promise in Christ Jesus through the gospel**.*
>
> *7 Of this gospel I have become a servant according to the gift of God's grace that was given me by the working of his power. 8 Although I am the very least of all the saints, this grace was given to me to bring to the Gentiles the news of the boundless riches of Christ, 9 and to make everyone see what is **the plan of the mystery hidden for ages in God** who created all things;*

*10 so that **through the church the wisdom of God in its rich variety might now be made known to the rulers and authorities in the heavenly places**.*

11 This was in accordance with the eternal purpose that he has carried out in Christ Jesus our Lord, 12 in whom we have access to God in boldness and confidence through faith in him.

13 I pray therefore that you may not lose heart over my sufferings for you; they are your glory. (Ephesians 3:1–13, NRSV)

Jesus is not coming back until this mystery has been fully revealed in the union of Jews and Gentiles together in the one body of Christ.

Ephesians 4:12–16

Ephesians 4 gives us another eschatological expectation. Here, Paul shows us that the ekklesia will grow up into full maturity prior to the end of history.

[The Spirit is] building up the body of Christ, until all of us come to the unity of the faith and of the knowledge of the Son of God, to maturity, to the measure of the full stature of Christ.

We must no longer be children, tossed to and fro and blown about by every wind of doctrine, by people's trickery, by their craftiness in deceitful scheming.

But speaking the truth in love, we must grow up in every way into him who is the head, into Christ, from whom the whole body, joined and knit together by every ligament with which it is equipped, as each part is working properly, promotes the body's growth in building itself up in love. (Ephesians 4:1–16, NRSV)

Has the church reached this sort of maturity? Not hardly. What does that say to us? Simply that Jesus will not return until his ekklesia is fully grown.

Colossians 1:15–20

We have strolled a path through Colossians 1 several times so far. But this time, let's look back at what Paul said with an eye on the question, "Is there a work here that must be completed before Jesus comes back?" Spoiler alert: The answer is yes.

Read the context again to get situated.

He is the image of the invisible God, the firstborn of all creation; for in him all things in heaven and on earth were created, things visible and invisible, whether thrones or dominions or rulers or powers —all things have been created through him and for him.

He himself is before all things, and in him all things hold together. He is the head of the body, the church; he is the beginning, the firstborn from the dead, so that he might come to have first place in everything.

For in him all the fullness of God was pleased to dwell, and through him God was pleased to reconcile to himself all things, whether on earth or in heaven, by making peace through the blood of his cross. (Colossians 1:15–20, NRSV)

We've already spent some time talking about how the same Christ who created "things visible and invisible, whether thrones or dominions or rulers or powers" has recreated them through his resurrection. But the point to emphasize here is *reconciliation:*

God was pleased to reconcile to himself all things, whether on earth or in heaven.

God reconciled all things to himself through death of Jesus. Yet Paul makes it clear that finished work of reconciliation is being finished through the ekklesia. Remember what Paul said in 2 Corinthians 5?

All this is from God, who reconciled us to himself through Christ, and has given us the ministry of reconciliation; that is, in Christ God was reconciling the world to himself, not counting their trespasses against them, and entrusting the message of reconciliation to us.

So we are ambassadors for Christ, since God is making his appeal through us; we entreat you on behalf of Christ, be reconciled to God. (2 Corinthians 5:18–20, NRSV)

The reconciliation of "things visible and invisible, whether thrones or dominions or rulers or powers" happens as we preach "the message of reconciliation," the good news of *"apokatastasis"* (universal restoration) that Peter preached in Acts 3.

Audacious Faith

What do all these texts tell us? There is work to be done. The victory of Christ's kingdom, the universal restoration of all things, the ministry of reconciliation, the *pleroma* of *ta ethne*, the completed temple, the full grown ekklesia—the everything we just worked through above!—cannot happen without us.

Christ descended to earth and then ascended back to heaven *for us*. He became incarnate so that we could be filled with all the fullness of God. He will not do the work of the kingdom without us.

And that realization requires audacious faith. It isn't hard to believe that Jesus could return and defeat evil once and for all. Of course, he could! But it takes audacious faith to believe that God can reconcile all things through fallen, frail, flawed humans like you and me.

It is easy to believe in the power of the Holy Spirit, for sure. But it is not so easy to believe in the power of the Holy Spirit *in you and me*. Humans seem to be the achilles heel of God's eternal purpose. God has a people problem, and we have a problem believing he can finish the work through us.

Read one final passage that drives home the point:

For this reason I bow my knees before the Father, from whom every family in heaven and on earth takes its name.

I pray that, according to the riches of his glory, he may grant that you may be **strengthened in your inner being with power through his Spirit***, and that* **Christ may dwell in your hearts through faith***, as you are being rooted and grounded in love.*

I pray that you may have the **power to comprehend***, with all the saints, what is the breadth and length and height and depth, and to know the love of Christ that surpasses knowledge, so* **that you may be filled with all the fullness of God***.*

Now to him who **by the power at work within us** *is* **able to accomplish abundantly far more than all we can ask or imagine***, to him be glory in the church and in Christ Jesus to all generations, forever and ever. Amen. (Ephesians 3:14–21, NRSV)*

God is able "accomplish abundantly far more than all we can ask or imagine" through his "power at work within us." Do you believe it?

UNIT 11: WHAT DO WE EXPECT? CORRECTING MISTAKEN ESCHATOLOGY

Christians have always explored various theories about how the world will end. In fact, apocalypticism is not unique to Christianity. People of all religious and even non-religious backgrounds have been fascinated by how it all ends. It seems that humans are born with a sense of eschatological fatalism. *"The end is coming!"* A quick browse through apocalyptic movies on Netflix will make that clear.

Truth be told, much of what we have studied on the kingdom so far cannot take root in our expectation until we root out mistaken eschatology. Unless you have already worked through similar teachings to what we've considered here, you have probably been twitching just a bit, dying to ask about the Mark of the Beast, the Great Tribulation, the Antichrist, the Rapture, the Millennium and how we all get to heaven when its all over.

You are not alone.

Yet there is a good reason for leaving all that until now—and even now we will not answer all your questions in full. There's just not enough time and space. But the reason for waiting until now to discuss traditional end times questions is simply that we need to see the big picture first. We need the background of Jesus' and Paul's teaching on the kingdom before we get into Revelation.

Revelation is explicitly written as apocalyptic literature, which means that it must be taken poetically and symbolically. In fact, the writer of Revelation tells us starting out that the book is written in symbols:

> *The revelation of Jesus Christ, which God gave him to show his servants what must soon take place;* **he made it known** *by sending his angel to his servant John. (Revelation 1:1, NRSV)*

The phrase "made it known" is from the Greek word *"semaino,"* which means "to signify." It literally means that the Book of Revelation is written in "sign language," symbolic language that conveys truth through symbols.

Revelation follows a long, centuries-old Jewish apocalyptic tradition where prophetic messages were conveyed in hidden symbols known only to the enlightened.

And that's why we must never use the apocalyptic symbols of Revelation to define how we interpret Jesus' and Paul's clear teaching. One of the fundamental rules of hermeneutics (the science of biblical interpretation) is that we must interpret the unclear by the plain, never the plain by the unclear.

Now, let's take a quick look at Revelation and related biblical material.

Revelation

There are four dominant views of the Book of Revelation:

1. Historicism: This view sees Revelation as fulfilled over the broad sweep of human history. This view became popular during the Protestant Reformation, but has fallen increasingly out of favor due to the expanding timeline and the difficulty of laying Revelation out over the span of continuing history.

2. Futurism: This view sees Revelation 4-22 as predicting future events. This perspective is most popular in American evangelicalism, particularly in the more fundamentalist traditions. (Dispensationalism, which has shaped much American eschatology, is a subset of futurism.)

3. Preterism: This view sees Revelation as a symbolic depiction of the destruction of Jerusalem in AD 70. Partial preterists believe that the Second Coming, the resurrection and judgment are all still future, while full preterists believe that all prophecy is fulfilled and the earth will continue forever, with believers going to heaven one-by-one as they die.

4. Idealism: This view doesn't hold to a literalist view of Revelation. Rather, it sees the book as a poetic description of what the struggle between good and evil will look like in every generation.

This is a fairly unusual point of view, but it does have some fervent adherents.

All of these views have been held with varying acceptance throughout Christian history. But, in reality, all the differing viewpoints have merely clouded the simple interpretation of Revelation.

Let's take a quick stab at it.

Revelation is best understood by studying the rest of the New Testament (as we've done) and then interpreting the cryptic, apocalyptic message of Revelation accordingly. And when we do so, something signifiant emerges: *the Book of Revelation is about the same thing as the rest of the New Testament.* The entire New Testament is about *the New Testament.* In other words, the entire New Testament is about *the New Covenant.*

The New Testament is about how the coming of Christ fulfilled the law and the prophets, how Jesus came to reveal the truth about the Father. The entire New Testament is about how the Old Covenant is reframed in light of the incarnation, resurrection and ascension of Jesus.

The New Testament sets out to explain how Israel's God is vindicated and proved faithful in spite of Israel's ongoing unfaithfulness and exile. How do we not judge God as a liar when all he promised in the law and prophets hasn't been fulfilled? That's what the New Testament is all about—explaining how Jesus is the fulfillment of the law and prophets in a new Christ-centered and Spirit-revealed way. Jesus is the interpretive lenses through which the Old Testament must be read. Otherwise, we get it all wrong.

Revelation is all about the same thing. It is all about the end of the Old Covenant age and the inauguration of the New Covenant age. If you'll back up and look at Revelation overall instead of bogging down for now in the symbols, you will see that it is all about the old temple/new temple, old city/new city, old bride/new bride, old priesthood/new priesthood, old age of angels/new age of sons and daughters. It is also about the destruction of the beasts (world empires, specifically Rome) that had persecuted the people of God.

One helpful way to understand Revelation is to sink down into Hebrews, reading it over and over until it oozes out your pores—and then read Revelation again. You will be amazed at how much the two books are saying the same thing:

> *In speaking of "a new covenant," he has made the first one obsolete. And what is obsolete and growing old will soon disappear. (Hebrews 8:13, NRSV)*

What was obsolete and growing old—that which would soon disappear—was the temple at Jerusalem and its system of worship. As Jesus had predicted in Matthew 24 (Mark 13, Luke 21), the city and temple would be destroyed as a sign that the old age had passed away and the new age of Messiah had come. The destruction of Jerusalem would be "the sign of the Son of Man in heaven" (Matthew 24:30), the sign that Jesus had ascended and was enthroned in heaven, as Daniel 7 foretold.

The destruction of Jerusalem was the single most significant geo-political event of the first century. It was like a thousand 9-11s. It was politically, militarily, religiously and spiritually earth-shattering. It was the end of the world—the end of the old world, the world of the Old Covenant age, the age of angels.

Much of the language in the New Testament that seems to describe the end of history, the end of the space-time continuum, is really just a poetic, symbolic way of describing the end of the old world and the birth of the new world.

For example, when Peter spoke of "the world that then was" that "perished" in the flood, he doesn't mean that the antediluvian world was actually another world. He means to say that the destruction of the earth was so complete that he could say that the old heavens and earth perished.

> *First of all you must understand this, that in the last days scoffers will come, scoffing and indulging their own lusts and saying, "Where is the promise of his coming? For ever since our ancestors died,*

all things continue as they were from the beginning of creation!"

They deliberately ignore this fact, that by the word of God heavens existed long ago and an earth was formed out of water and by means of water, through which **the world of that time was deluged with water and perished.** *But by* **the same word the present heavens and earth** *have been reserved for fire, being kept until the day of judgment and destruction of the godless. (2 Peter 3:3–7, NRSV)*

Just so, when Isaiah prophesied the destruction of Babylon, he used cosmic language to signify the fall of government and end of kingdoms.

For the stars of the heavens and their constellations will not give their light; the sun will be dark at its rising, and the moon will not shed its light. (Isaiah 13:10, NRSV)

When Peter quoted Joel prophesying the end of the world, he applied it to the first century proclaiming, "This is that!"

"And I will show portents in the heaven above and signs on the earth below, blood, and fire, and smoky mist. The sun shall be turned to darkness and the moon to blood, before the coming of the Lord's great and glorious day. Then everyone who calls on the name of the Lord shall be saved." (Acts 2:19–21, NRSV)

Was Joel predicting the end of the world? Yes, the end of the old world. It was the end of the Old Covenant age.

Revelation is about God's judgment upon Jerusalem, with its corrupted temple, and Rome, the beast the Daniel saw that was so terrible. The judgment of King Jesus on Jerusalem was a cosmic judgment on the *stoicheia*. It was a signal that the kingdom of God was coming into the world and that the nations of the earth must worship their true King.

(If you want to dig further into the details of Revelation, read *The Beast of Revelation* by J.D. King. You could also read *Victorious Eschatology* by Harold Eberle, among a thousand others. Ask for recommendations if you're interested.)

Here's a quick rundown of several key eschatological passages in the New Testament and how we should interpret them in light of the gospel of the kingdom:

• Daniel was fulfilled in the first century. The Seventy Weeks of Daniel and all that he foretold (with the exception of the resurrection predicted in Daniel 12) are already fulfilled.

• Matthew 24 (and parallels) were about AD 70, not the end of human history. These prophecies are some of the most powerful proofs of Christ's trustworthiness you will find.

- 1 Corinthians 15 is a passage about the future return of Christ after the powers are subdued under his feet.

- 1 Thessalonians 4 is a future prediction concerning Christ's return. We will go out to meet our King and escort him back to dwell forever within his living temple.

- 2 Thessalonians 1-2 is likely about Nero and the Roman Empire that was coming under judgment for its persecution of believers.

- 2 Peter 3 is most likely about AD 70 and the coming judgment upon Jerusalem.

- Revelation is about the end of the world—the *old world*. The book opens in a temple scene that defines the rest of the book. The entire book is about God's judgment on the corrupted earthly temple, the opening of the true temple in the heavens, and how the heavens shall break through upon the earth. Revelation is "the revelation of Jesus Christ" (Revelation 1:1) and how he is the earth's true King. World empires must bow before him.

Revelations opens with this:

The Revelation of Jesus Christ, which God gave unto him, to shew unto his servants **things which must shortly come to pass**; *and he sent and signified it by his angel unto his servant John. (Revelation 1:1, KJV)*

The things revealed in Revelation are things that would "shortly come to pass." Revelation then closes with this:

*And he said to me, "Do not seal up the words of the prophecy of this book, **for the time is near**." (Revelation 22:10, NRSV)*

This is in direct contrast to Daniel 12 where the angel instructed:

*"But you, Daniel, **keep the words secret and the book sealed until the time of the end**. Many shall be running back and forth, and evil shall increase." (Daniel 12:4, NRSV)*

*He said, "Go your way, Daniel, for **the words are to remain secret and sealed until the time of the end**." (Daniel 12:9, NRSV)*

Daniel was instructed to seal up his prophecy because it would take a long time (almost five centuries!) to be fulfilled. John was instructed *exactly the opposite*. Why? Because the time was near.

Revelation was fulfilled in the first century. The only prophecies in Revelation left to be fulfilled is the conquest of the nations (Revelation 19), the binding of Satan (Revelation 20) and the New Jerusalem fully manifest on earth in transformed culture (Revelation 21-22).

That changes everything.

UNIT 12: FINAL WORD

When we discover our place in the kingdom, we will discover the purpose for which we were created. Before time began, the triune God moved and brooded deep within his own eternal counsels. He was thinking, planning, dreaming. In the yearning of his everlasting love, he imagined you. He crafted you, shaped you, designed you, and then he held you deep within the womb of his purpose until the perfect time for your creative debut.

From the moment you emerged from your mother's womb, you embarked on a journey that God had mapped out for you and inscribed on heavenly scrolls, labeled with your name. You had no idea that your DNA was handcrafted to reflect the image of God in a way that no one else could. Your DNA is Spirit-programmed God-code.

The great Creator, in his genius, even adapted his purpose within you to accommodate your natural lineage. Though the iniquity of the generations into which you born tried to distort and misshape you, God was not surprised. He knew what you would face, and he planned for you to overcome.

He knew, though, that your eternal purpose required ignition by a divine spark, the gift of the Spirit that would awaken your latent true self hidden with Christ in God. He breathed his breath of life in you, and the true you was born from above.

The kingdom had come within you.

You were drawn by the Spirit into the Kingdom community, and the ekklesia baptized you into communion with the body of Christ. You were vested with kingdom authority, given keys to the kingdom, and recognized as a fully adopted child of God. You learned to worship, pray and serve.

But something within you kept crying out for more. You are a child of the kingdom, and empty religion soon could not satisfy. You were designed for purpose, birthed for purpose and saved for purpose. Nothing less than your eternal purpose could ever satisfy.

Then you heard the gospel of the kingdom. Your heart leapt within you, and your spirit became so alive with divine curiosity that it seemed as you were born again, again. Your pulse quickened, your bones burned, and you cried out with passion beyond words, "How can I serve the King in the release of his kingdom?"

As if he answered from heaven, you begin to hear from preachers you'd never known, singers you'd never heard, people you'd never met about the kingdom and how it comes in the world. You started learning about the ekklesia, built upon the rock, about the keys of the kingdom and deputized authority to serve in your assigned area of influence.

You came alive. Sunday worship—in fact, everyday worship!—became about glory encounters that transformed you and empowered you to carry the glory into your metron. The five-faceted ministry started releasing grace that equipped you as never before to influence others through love, wisdom and power. You found your field, and then you found your harvest.

Life is now filled with meaning. You know why you're here, why you're on the planet, why you've walked through the hell you've experienced. Everything you've been through has fine tuned your identity, broken off crippling lies that you'd believed. You started experiencing inner healing, and your prosperity of soul has begun manifesting as the prosperity of life.

The gifts of the Spirit are working in you now more than ever. And not just at church on Sunday. No, manifold Spirit-gifts have emerged effortlessly from your divine design, from the echoes of eternity that draw your soul back to who you were before time began. You are becoming the true you.

People around you have noticed the change. They have been drawn inexorably to your unreligious, easy fellowship with God and people. They love that you live without guilt and shame, modeling goodness and godliness without being churchy or preachy. You are not offended by their sin. They do not sense judgment coming from, but just an easy acceptance without compromise.

Your metron has been changing. The kingdom is coming in the world through you. Not only are the people in your sphere being influenced by your love, wisdom and power, but the powers that have dominated your neighborhood and workplace are beginning to shrink back from the strategic, prophetic intercession that you have learned to release.

You are learning to wield the authority you carry. You have learned the power of persevering prayer. You have learned to cast out demons and bind the strongman. You have learned how to release angel armies. You found your seat in the Divine Council. You heal the sick, speak life to the oppressed and deliver the captives. The kingdom of God is taking root in *your* world through *your* influence. You never imagined life could be this meaningful. But the gospel of the kingdom has changed your world.

Changed people change the world.

Would you like for this story (individually tailored to you, of course!) to be your story? Read it again, and then write out your story as if you were at the end of your life telling people what it was like to be you. Imagine with God. Dream with him. He created you for an eternal purpose. Don't die until you find it!

You will find that this eternal purpose is embedded within the gospel of the kingdom. Seek first the kingdom, and all these other things will be added to you.

www.ingramcontent.com/pod-product-compliance
Lightning Source LLC
Chambersburg PA
CBHW030859170426
43193CB00009BA/670